John's Gospel

D0993833

In this innovative book on *John's Gospel*, Mark W.G. Stibbe introduces a wide readership to a number of literary approaches to the fourth gospel. He examines the character of Jesus using reader response criticism, the plot using structuralist literary criticism and the genre using archetypal criticism. The style is analysed using the methodology of narrative criticism. Dr Stibbe interprets the polemic against the Jews by drawing on the ethics of reception.

In addition, *John's Gospel* includes an introduction which puts readers in touch with recent research, and a conclusion which points forward to future areas of development. There is also a comprehensive bibliography.

This book will appeal to theologians, students of Divinity and ministers of religion, as well as to all those who are interested in the Bible as literature.

Mark W.G. Stibbe is the Vicar of St Mark's at Grenoside in Sheffield and an Honorary Lecturer in the Department of Biblical Studies at the University of Sheffield. He is the author of several books about St John, and is Chairman of the Johannine Seminar at the British New Testament Conference.

New Testament Readings

Edited by John Court
University of Kent at Canterbury

John's Gospel

Mark W.G. Stibbe

London and New York

First published 1994
by Routledge
11 New Fetter Lane, London EC4P 4EE

Simultaneously published in the USA and Canada
by Routledge
29 West 35th Street, New York, NY 10001

Typeset in Baskerville by
Ponting–Green Publishing Services, Chesham, Bucks
Printed and bound in Great Britain by
T.J. Press (Padstow) Ltd, Padstow, Cornwall.

Printed on acid free paper

British Library Cataloguing in Publication Data
A catalogue record for this book is available from the
British Library.

Library of Congress Cataloging-in-Publication Data.
Stibbe, Mark W.G.
    John's Gospel / Mark W.G. Stibbe.
        p.   cm. – (New Testament readings)
    Includes bibliographical references.
        1. Bible. N.T. John–Criticism, interpretation, etc.
2. Bible as literature   I. Title.   II. Series.
BS2615.2.S745   1994
226.5'066–dc20   94–7478

ISBN 0–415–09510–7 (hbk)   0–415–09511–5 (pbk)

To Andrew and Carol Lincoln

Contents

Series editor's preface

This volume has every right to stand on its own, as a significant contribution to the study of the book of the New Testament with which it is concerned. But equally it is a volume in a series entitled *New Testament Readings*. Each volume in this series deals with an individual book among the early Christian writings within, or close to the borders of, the New Testament. The series is not another set of traditional commentaries, but designed as a group of individual interpretations or 'readings' of the texts, offering fresh and stimulating methods of approach. While the contributors may be provocative in their choice of a certain perspective, they also seek to do justice to a range of modern methods and provide a context for the study of each particular text.

The collective object of the series is to share with the widest readership the extensive range of recent approaches to Scripture. There is no doubt that literary methods have presented what amounts to a 'new look' to the Bible in recent years. But we should not neglect to ask some historical questions or apply suitable methods of criticism from the Social Sciences. The origins of this series are in a practical research programme at the University of Kent, with an inclusive concern about ways of using the Bible. It is to be hoped that our series will offer fresh insights to all who, for any reason, study or use these books of the early Christians.

John M. Court
Series Editor

Acknowledgements

Throughout this book I have used the New International Version of the Bible (London: Hodder and Stoughton, 1987 edition) and the third edition of Kurt Aland's *Greek New Testament* (United Bible Societies). I am grateful to have had access to both texts.

In Chapter 2 I have included a radically revised version of an article entitled 'Return to Sender: A Structuralist Approach to John's Gospel', published in *Biblical Interpretation* 1, Pt 2, 1993, pp. 189–206. I am grateful to Dr Mark Brett, one of the executive editors of that journal, for permission to reproduce parts of it here.

I would also like to thank Dr John Court (editor of this Routledge series) and Richard Stoneman at Routledge for their help, encouragement and support.

The same goes for the post-graduate seminar group at the Department of Biblical Studies at Sheffield University for their challenging and helpful criticisms of the first draft of Chapter 5, which was presented as a paper in October 1993. Their incisive responses helped to refine the argument.

Finally, I would like to place on record the debt I owe to my friend and colleague Dr Andrew Lincoln. Over the last ten years, many of the ideas which I have had about John's gospel have first been discussed with Andrew over an Indian curry or a pint of ale. He has been an invaluable dialogue partner during that time, and at least some of my insights into this magnificent gospel have taken shape as a result of his stimulating comments. I feel that it is therefore only appropriate that this fourth book which I have written on John should be dedicated to my friends, Andrew and Carol.

Introduction

There is a literary device used frequently in the fourth gospel known as *inclusio*. This is a technique whereby the author ends a text in a manner reminiscent of its beginning. It is a device which gives the impression of circularity, of a narrative coming full circle.

John's gospel contains many examples of *inclusio*, both in its individual episodes and in the gospel as a whole. There is, for example, an *inclusio* between John 20 and John 1. In John 20.15, the risen Jesus appears at the tomb and asks Mary Magdalene 'Who is it you are looking for?' In Greek, the question is *Tina zeteis*. This reminds the alert reader of the very first words of Jesus to the two disciples in John 1.38: 'What are you looking for?' which, in the Greek, is *Ti zeteite*. In both contexts, the key-word *zetein* ('to look for; to seek') is used. A distant *inclusio* is therefore established.

It is an odd coincidence that studies of the fourth gospel during the twentieth century exhibit a kind of *inclusio*. In the first few decades, one of the most popular approaches to John was that of comparative literary criticism. Scholars like Hitchcock (1911, 1923) and Windisch (1923) examined the fourth gospel as literature, often drawing comparisons with classical Greek tragedy. So prevalent was this literary approach to the Bible as a whole between 1900 and 1930, that C.H. Dodd could write in 1928 that 'The widespread appreciation of the Bible as literature is, indeed, one of the most salutary results of the general change of outlook in the last two generations' (1928: 2).

Between 1930 and 1970, however, literary approaches to the fourth gospel almost entirely disappeared. Occasional studies of the structure, unity and dramatic qualities of the gospel did emerge, but by and large the study of the fourth gospel was dominated by German source criticism. Rudolf Bultmann, whose magisterial commentary on John was originally published in 1941, is a particularly important figure in this regard. Instead of treating the gospel as a literary and stylistic unity, Bultmann – and many influenced by him – pointed to the flaws in the narrative, to the *aporiae* or interruptions to the flow of the story. These, Bultmann argued, provide evidence that the gospel is the product of at least two different authors, the second of whom ('the ecclesiastical redactor') has clumsily added other traditional pericopae, displaced existing material, and inserted his own theological interpretation.

Not surprisingly, the kind of literary appreciation of the fourth gospel which had emerged at the turn of the century now receded. If the fourth gospel was not an artistic unity but a patchwork quilt of different sources, then it was not easy to see how anyone could analyse it as literature. However, at the beginning of the 1970s, scholars began to question this. A number of writers had already made the point that the fourth gospel exhibits a remarkably consistent literary style (Schweizer 1939; Ruckstuhl 1951). Others began to argue that John's sources are not as visible as Bultmann and others were maintaining. Some argued that in stories like the raising of Lazarus (John 11.1–44), John's style is so consistent that it is impossible to differentiate between the author and his source material (Lindars 1971).

At the same time as this critique of source criticism began to surface, a new movement of literary appreciation also began. In 1970, David Wead published his dissertation, *The Literary Devices in the Fourth Gospel*. In 1973, George MacRae published an influential article on 'Theology and Irony in the Fourth Gospel'. Towards the end of the 1970s, Marinus de Jonge began to look at the fourth gospel as a literary unity. Frank Kermode included a post-modern literary analysis on John's passion narrative in his book, *Genesis of Secrecy* (1979). In 1979, John Dominic Crossan produced the first proper attempt at a structuralist literary analysis of the gospel ('A Structuralist Analysis of John 6').

As the 1970s drew to a close, the scene was set for a scholarly *inclusio* – a return, in the last few decades of the century, to the Johannine literary criticism which had dominated the first few decades. This is precisely what has happened. The present scene in fourth gospel research is now dominated by literary approaches to John. They are the methods which represent fresh approaches and which are yielding new insights. However, there is an important difference between the situation today and the situation between

1900 and 1930. Then the standard literary approaches were either dramatic or structural. In other words, literary critics either looked at the dramatic qualities of John's gospel (usually comparing it to Attic tragedy) or they attempted to uncover the literary design and structure of the narrative. Today, however, there is a much greater variety of methodologies. Structuralism, deconstructive criticism, feminist literary criticism, narrative criticism, reader response criticism, rhetorical criticism, speech act theory and discourse analysis all jostle for pole position in the hermeneutical pluralism of our time. No one method has forged ahead. All are used to highlight the literary characteristics of the fourth gospel.

In this book I want to introduce the reader to a variety of literary readings of the fourth gospel. In Chapter 1 ('Hero') I will begin with a reader response approach to John's characterization of Jesus. In this chapter, I will show how the one sent down from heaven is not a redeemer who is easily grasped either at the intellectual or at the physical level. Rather, he plays the part of a kind of first century Scarlet Pimpernel. He constantly evades the attempts of the hostile Jerusalem authorities to arrest him. He equally often seems to evade the comprehension of his listeners. He is quintessentially an elusive Messiah.

In Chapter 2 ('Plot') we move from a reader response approach to a structuralist analysis of John's plot. I have summarized the story of John's gospel using Elvis Presley's song title, 'Return to Sender'. This perfectly encapsulates the overall shape and movement of John's plot. Jesus is the one sent down to earth by the Father, who accomplishes the Father's work here on earth, and then returns to the heavenly Sender at the end of the story. Such a plot seems to me to be tailor-made for a structuralist analysis. A.J. Greimas' actantial approach to narrative plots uses terms like Sender and Receiver. I will use his terminology in this second chapter.

In Chapter 3 ('Genre'), I want to move from this structuralist description of John's plot to an archetypal investigation of its genre. So far the study of the genre of the fourth gospel has been a relatively neglected area. The few scholars who have devoted attention to this topic have tried to argue that John's gospel is closest in form and content to ancient *Bios* (biography). I agree with this basic description. However, in Chapter 3 I want to go further than this. As a supplementary approach, I will take Northrop Frye's analysis of *mythoi* or 'plot-types' and map the plot of the fourth gospel against his four archetypal stories in literature: the *mythos* of spring (comedy), the *mythos* of summer (romance), the *mythos* of autumn (tragedy) and the *mythos* of winter (satire). We shall find that this method, which is principally focused upon John's plot, goes a great deal further in explaining the classic appeal of John's gospel than the few recent studies which see the gospel simply as a *Bios Iesou*.

In the fourth chapter I will look at the 'style' of the fourth gospel and try to show how and why John's gospel has such an abiding appeal. In this chapter I will examine one text (John 11.1–44) using the method of narrative criticism. Here I will describe the way in which the author uses context, setting, time, character, narrator, form, structure, irony, symbolism, focus, and other devices in order to achieve the rhetorical purpose announced in John 20.31: to persuade the reader that Jesus is the Christ, the Son of God, and that in him we can experience eternal life. In this chapter I will therefore try to highlight the major stylistic features of John's narrative art, thereby giving readers the analytic tools with which to study other stories for themselves.

In the final chapter on 'polemic' I want to look at the use of satire in the fourth gospel. Using a new literary approach called 'the ethics of reception', I want to examine John's use of satire, particularly his satire directed against the Jews. This aspect of the fourth gospel undoubtedly presents a problem to any contemporary reader with a concern for Jewish-Christian dialogue and for justice for the Jewish people. We will therefore examine what looks like the most violent of these polemics, John 8.31–59, and expose it to a literary-ethical reading in order to assess what value and relevance this kind of polemic has today.

This book therefore has a twofold purpose. My first purpose is to introduce a wide readership to the aesthetic qualities of the fourth gospel. My second purpose is to introduce the same readers to the different literary approaches which can be profitably applied to John's story. Thus, Chapter 1 on the 'Hero' uses the approach of reader response criticism. Chapter 2 on 'Plot' uses structuralism. Chapter 3 on 'Genre' uses archetypal criticism. Chapter 4 on 'Style' uses narrative criticism. Chapter 5 on 'Polemic' uses a literary-ethical approach. It is my sincere hope that these short studies will help many readers to rediscover the riches of a narrative which presents a searching world with *aletheia*, 'reality!'

Chapter 1

Hero

One of the stories which most excited me as a child was Baroness Orczy's novel, *The Scarlet Pimpernel*. This is not a great work of literature; it is simply a fast-moving adventure story about an English count who travels over to Paris during the Reign of Terror. His mission is to rescue French aristocrats who have been sentenced to death at the hands of Madame Guillotine. Many adventures ensue in which the hero manages to elude the city authorities and to snatch their victims from the jaws of death. To these authorities he is a slippery and evasive man, constantly fooling them with cunning disguises, constantly thwarting their desperate attempts to apprehend him. Indeed, the hero – known as 'the Pimpernel' – taunts them with a piece of doggerel: 'They seek him here, they seek him there, those Frenchies seek him everywhere. Is he in heaven? Is he in hell? That damned elusive Pimpernel!'

Quite a few years after my final reading of this novel I started studying the gospel of John. Initially my encounters with this gospel were dictated by the readings which were, at the time, dominant in the universities. These readings were exclusively diachronic and atomistic. That is, they encouraged students to examine individual pericopae (passages) with a view to the archaeological exhumation of the sources, traditions, religious influences and redaction supposedly behind each text. Having been brought up by a father who was tutored by C.S. Lewis, and having studied English literature as my first degree, I not unnaturally baulked at such an approach. Too much of the artistry, the excitement, the mystery of John's story seemed to me to be destroyed by the various methodologies associated with historical criticism.

In the early 1980s, I began to rebel against this demystifying and anti-aesthetic trend in fourth gospel research. I set about reading the whole of the gospel as a story told by a skilful author. In this endeavour, a profound turning-point occurred when I heard an actor reading the whole of the gospel. On a long car journey I listened to the entire gospel on an audio cassette. In the process I was captivated by the character of Jesus as the hero of the story. Here was a man who was both divine and human, who had come down from heaven to his own people, who was largely unrecognized, misunderstood and persecuted, and who was consequently forced to play a game of hide-and-seek throughout the story. Here was a man who seemed to me the archetype of the elusive hero.

What struck me as I listened to John's gospel were the distant resonances with Orczy's *Scarlet Pimpernel.* Of course, the two stories are worlds apart, but broad similarities do exist. Like Orczy's hero, the Johannine Jesus is on a salvific quest; not a quest to rescue aristocrats but a much more democratic quest to save humanity. Like Orczy's hero, the Johannine Jesus is pitted against urban authorities; not the revolutionary tribunal of seventeenth-century Paris but the Jewish authorities in first century Jerusalem. Above all, like Orczy's hero, the Johannine Jesus is thoroughly elusive; not elusive in terms of disguise, but elusive in terms of movement (constantly evading capture) and language (constantly mystifying his interlocutors). Indeed, what strikes me today is the resemblance between Orczy's hero and what one might call the 'Johannine Pimpernel' – Jesus of Nazareth. As far as the latter is concerned, I have somewhat frivolously created my own jingle: 'They seek him here, they seek him there, those Jews, they seek him everywhere!'

In teaching the fourth gospel either in universities or in the church, I now begin by trying to help people to appreciate these characteristics of John's hero. It is for this reason that I want to begin this book with a study of John's characterization of Jesus. This is the obvious place to start; Jesus is clearly the main subject of the fourth gospel. As Richard Burridge remarks, 'Over half of the verbs are taken up with Jesus' deeds or words, performed or spoken by him (55.3%)' (1992: 223).

READER RESPONSE CRITICISM

So important is our ability to engage with John's enigmatic hero that I want to give the reader a brief tour through the whole gospel, showing at every point how the author tells his story with the controlling theme of the recondite Christ in mind. What I want to offer is a reading of the fourth gospel which highlights John's portrayal of his hero as the hidden Messiah. Before we begin, however, one question must be answered. What kind of methodology will we use?

The most appropriate method is the method of reader response criticism pioneered by Wolfgang Iser. In his book, *The Implied Reader*, Iser outlines some of the main features of this phenomenological approach to a work of literature. What concerns Iser are 'the actions involved in responding to that text', to the ways in which a literary text is 'realized' (1974: 274). He is not primarily concerned with the artistic elements of a text; that is, the literary qualities inherent in the text. He is concerned with the aesthetic elements; that is, the responses engendered by the text in the reader. The reason for this is simple. In Iser's view, a work of literature does not live on its own. It only lives when it is realized by a reader. The text comes to life in the convergence of text and reader. In this convergence, there is an awakening of responses in the reader and it is then that the text lives.

Iser's conviction is that authors create literary texts which are designed to engage the imagination of the reader. He cites Laurence Sterne's remarks in *Tristram Shandy*:

> The truest respect which you can pay to the reader's understanding, is to halve this matter amicably, and leave him something to imagine, in his turn, as well as yourself. For my own part, I am eternally paying him compliments of this kind, and do all that lies in my power to keep his imagination as busy as my own.
>
> (Iser 1974: 275)

Iser uses these words to propose that a text is 'an arena in which reader and author participate in a game of the imagination' (op. cit. p.275). He argues that an author never tries to tell the whole story in which everything is laid out cut and dried before us. That would eliminate the pleasurable side of reading altogether. Instead, the author creates a text with an unwritten part which stimulates the imagination into creative activity. He cites Virginia Woolf's comment about Jane Austen, an author who 'stimulates us to supply what is not there' (op. cit. p.275). All good authors, argues Iser, try to stimulate us to supply what is not 'there'.

Iser is aware that there is a danger of subjectivism in trying to describe the actual processes involved in this psychology of reading. Nevertheless, he boldly goes where no critic has gone before and attempts to outline some of the main characteristics of what he calls the reading process. One of Iser's most important insights is his emphasis on the imagination. The imagination, as many philosophers have pointed out, is the synthetic faculty in the human mind. It works hand in hand with memory, attempting to synthesize remembered phenomena into new and complex relations. Put another way, the imagination creates connections between the many different phenomena experienced by the senses and stored in one's memory.

In the matter of reading texts, 'Whatever we have read sinks into our memory and is foreshortened' (op. cit. p.278). Later on, what we have read may be evoked again against a different background, 'with the result that the reader is enabled to develop hitherto unforeseeable connections' (278). As this happens, the reader 'actually causes the text to reveal its potential multiplicity of connections' (op. cit. p.278). The text itself leaves what Iser calls 'gaps'. These 'inevitable omissions' (op. cit. p.280) are what gives a story its dynamism. When readers come to the text, the opportunity is given for us to bring into play our own faculty for establishing connections. 'The reader will strive, even if unconsciously, to fit everything together in a consistent pattern' (op. cit. p.283). Reading is therefore an act of re-creation:

> We look forward, we look back, we decide, we change our decisions, we form expectations, we are shocked by their non-fulfilment, we question, we muse, we accept, we reject; this is the dynamic process of recreation.
>
> (Iser 1974: 288)

READING JOHN'S STORY OF JESUS

Iser's contributions are essential for our reading of the fourth gospel. For too long, reading John has involved a positivistic detachment of subject and object. The diachronic reader (subject) has stood over the text (object) with all the pseudo-scientific objectivity and superiority associated with the dark side of the Enlightenment. However, in Iser's paradigm, this subject-object division is rejected. What replaces it is a philosophy of participation. 'Text and reader no longer confront each other as object and subject' (op. cit. p.293). What is important now is that the reader fully participates in the story, filling in the gaps which have inevitably been left by the author.

Iser's theory of reception has particular ramifications for our response to John's characterization of Jesus. In the case of John's portrayal of his hero, the active participation of the reader is essential because there are many 'gaps' in the story. This is not something which we find easy to assimilate; the 'modern mind' is used to the detailed characterization which we find in the eighteenth, nineteenth and twentieth century English novel. In novels such as *Emma* or *Tess*, the narrator provides a very precise commentary on the interior thoughts, motives and attitudes of major characters. We are given the privilege of entering the hero's 'stream of consciousness'. In the fourth gospel, however, this kind of internal commentary is very rare. The narrator tells us very little of Jesus' thoughts, motives and attitudes. We are only given occasional, fragmented and laconic glimpses, such as the following:

2.24: Jesus would not entrust himself to them, because he knew all men.

5.6: When Jesus saw him lying there and learned that he had been in this condition for a long time, he asked him, 'Do you want to get well?'

6.6: He asked this only to test him, for he already had in mind what he was going to do.

6.15: Jesus, knowing that they intended to come and make him king by force, withdrew again to a mountain by himself.

6.61: Aware that his disciples were grumbling about this, Jesus said to them . . .

7.1: After this, Jesus went around in Galilee, purposely staying away from Judea because the Jews there were waiting to take his life.

7.39: By this he meant the Spirit . . .

11.5: Jesus loved Martha and her sister and Lazarus.

11.33: When Jesus saw her weeping, and the Jews who had come along with her also weeping, he was deeply moved in spirit and troubled.

11.38: Jesus, once more deeply moved, came to the tomb.

12.33: He said this to show the kind of death he was going to die.

13.1:   Jesus knew that the time had come for him to leave this world and go the Father.

13.3:   Jesus knew that the Father had put all things under his power.

13.11: For he knew who was going to betray him.

13.21: After he had said this, Jesus was troubled in spirit and testified . . .

16.19: Jesus saw that they wanted to ask him about this, so he said to them . . .

18.4:   Jesus, knowing all that was going to happen to him, went out and asked them . . .

19.28: Later, knowing that all was now completed, and so that the Scripture would be fulfilled, Jesus said . . .

21.19: Jesus said this to indicate the kind of death by which Peter would glorify God.

To a reader familiar with the psychological explanations present in novelistic fiction, such asides are likely to be deemed frugal at best. However, modern readers must make certain adjustments when reading narratives so obviously influenced by ancient Hebrew narrative techniques. Thanks to Robert Alter's excellent 1981 study, *The Art of Biblical Narrative*, we now know a good deal more about how the ancient Biblical authors composed stories. Alter's chapter on characterization shows how in the Old Testament we have to infer the character of a figure like Samson or David from one of the following: first of all, from the narrator's description of their actions, appearance or attitudes; second, from the comments made by another character about them; third, from their direct speech; fourth, from their interior monologue or inward speech (Alter 1981: 116–117). Alter places these four means of inferring character on a kind of spectrum of certainty. At one end (narrator's description of actions, attitudes and appearances) we can make inferences which are not altogether certain. At the other end (interior monologue), we can be much more certain in our analysis of character.

For readers of the modern novel the principal difficulty with Hebrew characterization is that characters rarely indulge in inward speech. As Shimon Bar-Efrat writes, in the Bible 'the narrator

makes very few direct statements about the characters' personalities' (1989: 89); there is by and large a reticence in relation to
'inward speech'. Old Testament narrators are 'omniscient but far
from omnicommunicative' (Sternberg 1985: 190). They leave a
great deal to the reader's imagination; they do not 'linger on
mental processes' but require the reader to infer such processes
'from externals alone' (Sternberg 1985: 191). The result is that the
reader is forced 'to get at character and motive through a process
of inference from fragmentary data, often with crucial pieces of
narrative exposition strategically withheld' (Alter 1981: 126).

All this is germane to the task of responding to John's hero, Jesus
of Nazareth. Iser argues that the reading process is an imaginative
filling in of gaps left by the author. Sternberg argues that biblical
narrative is 'a system of gaps that must be filled in' (1985: 186).
The same is true of John's gospel. John is not a modern novel but
a story told in the Hebrew style of storytelling. It is a system of gaps
that must be filled in by the reader. As in Hebrew narrative, in
John's gospel we have to infer Jesus' character principally from his
actions and direct speech. This means that we need to see John's
portrayal of Jesus as continuous with Hebrew narrative art (Staley
1991: 55–58). There is a certain urgency about this, for whilst there
has been a lot of work done on John's use of the Old Testament,
there has been little written about John's use of Old Testament
narrative techniques.

In what follows, I will look at each of the major sections of the
fourth gospel and examine the characterization of Jesus from the
perspective of reader-response criticism. The sections of the gospel
can be divided up as follows:

PART I: John 1–12. THE MINISTRY OF JESUS

John 1:   The Prologue and Introduction

John 2–4:   The first itinerary of Jesus

John 5–10:   The second itinerary of Jesus

John 11–12:   The Conclusion

PART II: John 13–21. THE DEPARTURE OF JESUS

John 13–17:   The Farewell

John 18–19:   The Passion

John 20–21:   The Resurrection

JOHN 1: A READER RESPONSE

The first chapter of the gospel serves as an introduction to the whole. It is composed of a prologue (vv.1–18) and four short episodes (vv.19–51). We will concentrate on the following three facets of Jesus' characterization in this chapter:

1 The narrator's first words about Jesus (John 1.1–5);
2 Jesus' first appearance in the narrative (1.26);
3 The first words of Jesus in the gospel (1.38). In all three cases we will find that Iser's reader-response methodology helps to under-line the elusiveness of John's protagonist.

We start, then, with the narrator's first words about Jesus. The narrator begins the gospel story with this famous declaration,

> In the beginning was the Word, and the Word was with God, and the Word was God. He was with God in the beginning. Through him all things were made; without him nothing was made that has been made. In him was life, and that life was the light of men. The light shines in the darkness, but the darkness has not understood it.
>
> (John 1.1–5)

Readers familiar with these words are apt to pass over them quickly, forgetting their strangeness for readers unfamiliar with the gospel and with the early church's debates concerning the Logos (Jesus the Word). However, reader-response criticism helps to defamiliar-ize this overture and to remind readers how strange it really is.

To help us glimpse something of the abstruseness of John's prologue, here are some comments from Meir Sternberg about the first verse of the Book of Genesis ('In the beginning God created ...') which have so obviously influenced the first words of the fourth gospel. Sternberg writes:

> The most startling thing about the Bible's opening words, 'When God began to create heaven and earth', is that God comes on stage with a complete absence of preliminaries. Who is God? What is God? Where does he hail from? How does he differ from other deities?
>
> (Sternberg 1985: 322)

What Sternberg says about Genesis 1.1 could equally well be said of John 1.1: The most startling thing about John's opening words,

'In the beginning was the Word', is that the Word comes on stage with a complete absence of preliminaries. Who is the Word? What is the Word? Where does he hail from? How does he differ from other deities?

What Sternberg's commentary reveals is the way in which the narrator of Genesis 1 withholds information, avoids direct characterization, and builds a sense of God's character only by degrees and only through speech and action. It is up to the reader to fill in the gaps and to synthesize the written and the unwritten into a coherent portrait of God.

What is true of God in Genesis 1 is true of the Word in John 1. Here again, the narrator makes demands upon the reader. The narrator is somewhat evasive. He introduces a figure described as *ho Logos* 'without preliminaries'. Indeed, the figure himself (*Logos* is masculine) is presented as a somewhat shadowy character. We will not know that 'the Word' is actually a title for Jesus Christ until verse 17, the first time that the name of Jesus is mentioned. Until then, the first-time reader may be kept guessing. 'What is the Word? Who is the Word?'

So there is a certain abstruseness about the narrator's portrayal of Jesus right from the very start of the story. This abstruseness is given further emphasis in the crucial statement in John 1.5: 'The light shines in the darkness, but the darkness has not understood it'. Here a vital clue is given concerning the characterization of the hero of the gospel. The hero is the light of the world (see John 8.12). He shines in the darkness, but the darkness has not understood it. 'Understood' is not a very satisfactory translation of the verb *katalambano*, as used in this context. A much better translation would be 'grasped', which has a connotation of both apprehension (grasping someone with one's hands) and comprehension (understanding someone with one's mind). Jesus is depicted as a hero who is not 'grasped' by the dark forces of the *kosmos*.

This judgement about the Word is important. Right at the outset, the narrator guides the reader into an understanding of Jesus as an enigmatic figure. He is introduced as an enigmatic figure in verses 1 to 4 of the prologue. He is then actually presented in terms of elusiveness in verse 5. Jesus is here depicted as a hero whom the forces of darkness will try to overcome and to understand (the two common translations of *katalambano* in 1.5). However, Jesus will evade these attempts until the hour arrives when he willingly gives himself into the hands of evil men. Until that time, people will seek

Jesus, both geographically and intellectually, but they will not necessarily find him. The heavenly pimpernel will not be manipulated or controlled by the political or the ecclesiastical authorities of this world. We, the readers, have been warned!

After the powerful words of the omniscient (but by no means omnicommunicative) narrator in the prologue, we now come to four short episodes:

John 1.19–28: First witness of the Baptist

John 1.29–34: Second witness of the Baptist

John 1.35–42: First witness of Jesus

John 1.43–51: Second witness of Jesus

In the first two episodes, the Baptist witnesses to the coming of Jesus in the presence of the priests and Levites from Jerusalem (1.19–28) and in the presence of an unspecified audience (1.29–34). In the second two episodes, Jesus witnesses to Andrew, Peter and an unnamed disciple (1.35–42), and then to Nathanael (1.43–51). What is of particular interest, as far as our reader response is concerned, is the first appearance of Jesus in 1.26, and the first words of Jesus in 1.38.

In the first episode after the prologue (1.19–28), John the Baptist is the protagonist. He is portrayed as a faithful witness, the voice calling out in the desert in preparation for the Messiah. The priests and Levites interrogate him, asking 'Are you the Messiah, or Elijah, or the Prophet?' But the Baptist replies, 'I am not'. 'Why, then, do you baptize people?' they ask. Here is the Baptist's enigmatic answer:

'I baptise with water but among you stands one you do not know. He is the one who comes after me, the thongs of whose sandals I am not worthy to untie.'

(John 1.26–27)

The attentive reader should, at this point, react with a certain surprise. There is someone present in the audience whom the Jewish envoys do not recognize. There is, to use Muilenburg's phrase, an 'Unknown One' in their midst (cited in Stibbe 1993b: 71). The Messiah is present incognito, and the priests and Levites – the religious representatives – cannot even see him! The first appearance of Jesus is therefore a mysterious appearance, designed to enhance a sense of his elusiveness in the mind of the attentive reader. 'Who does he mean?' 'Where is this person?' 'How do we spot him?' the reader asks.

The first words of Jesus in John's gospel have a similar recondite connotation. They are recorded in John 1.38, where Jesus turns round and asks the two disciples who are following him, 'What do you want?' The verb in the Greek is *zetein*, 'to seek'. These words have the sense of a quest. 'What are you two seeking after?' Alan Culpepper rightly comments that 'his [Jesus'] first words are a question whose meaning can be extended to existential depths' (1983: 108). They are important because they alert the reader at the earliest stage to one of the primary motifs of the gospel, which is 'seeking Jesus', an action which the narrator presents as the ultimate religious quest (John 14.6).

The verb *zetein* is used thirty-four times in John. One quarter of the usages of this verb in the New Testament are to be found in the fourth gospel. However, only on three occasions does a character who seeks Jesus actually find him; here in 1.41 and 1.45, and once more in 6.25. The reason for this is because there is a 'hide-and-seek' dynamic going on in John's story. People seek after Jesus, but he (as we shall see) constantly hides from them. Sometimes this concealment is expressed in the direct speech of Jesus. He hides or conceals himself from people through his cryptic and evasive use of words. At other times this concealment is expressed in the actions of Jesus. Here he literally hides from those who are looking for him.

The significance of Jesus' first words are this: they warn the reader of the constant seeking after Jesus that will take place throughout the entire story. Here, Andrew and Philip are lucky. They are allowed to 'find' Jesus (1.41; 1.45). From this moment on, many others will not be so privileged. They will find Jesus abstrusive, sometimes even offensive. They will not be invited to 'remain' with Jesus (1.38–39).

JOHN 2–4: A READER RESPONSE

There is a good deal of material in John 1 which reinforces the impression of Jesus' elusive character. This elusiveness is, by and large, evoked by what the narrator leaves unsaid, a tactic which forces the reader to ask questions like:

Who is the Word? (1.1)

Why can the darkness not grasp him? (1.5)

Why did the world not recognize him? (1.10)

Why does Jesus conceal himself? (1.26)

Why do we not see or hear Jesus in 1.29–34?

Where is Jesus staying? (1.39)

When and how did Jesus see Nathanael? (1.48)

We shall find that these omissions or 'gaps' are a feature of the next section of the gospel as well. This second section extends from John 2.1 to John 4.54.

The section opens with a lively story set in Cana at Galilee. The events take place at a wedding reception in which the wine runs out. At this point, Jesus' mother makes a request to her son, expressed in the form of a leading statement: 'They have no more wine' (John 2.3). Jesus, rather surprisingly, replies with a rebuke: 'Dear woman, why do you involve me? My time has not yet come' (2.4). However, Jesus' mother somewhat resiliently ignores the rebuke and turns to the servants and says, 'Do whatever he tells you' (2.5). Jesus then responds to his mother's initial request by transforming up to 180 gallons of water into the same amount of fine wine. The story ends with the comic surprise of the head waiter (2.9–10), and with the narrator's description of the miracle as 'the first of Jesus' signs' (2.11).

In this story, the abstrusiveness of Jesus emerges from his speech and actions. Particularly striking are the gaps or ellipses in the logic of the conversation. The mother of Jesus comes to her son with news about the lack of wine, and Jesus replies with a rather enigmatic rebuke. The reader, at this point, wants to know why Jesus is so terse with his own mother. Why should the fact that Jesus' hour has not yet come affect his ability or desire to perform a miracle? Why is he reluctant to oblige? The next comment, made by the mother of Jesus, seems a total *non sequitur.* Having been told off, she turns to the waiters and says, 'Do whatever he tells you.' This implies that Jesus has accepted the invitation to provide wine for the guests. We, the readers, might justly ask, 'When and how did that occur?' All along Jesus' words and actions are mysterious. We are left to fill in the gaps between the request, the rebuke and the response ourselves. The narrator never explains why Jesus' intitial reluctance turns so quickly to acquiescence.

Directly after this, the narrator includes one of a number of itinerary fragments:

After this, he went down to Capernaum with his mother and brothers and his disciples. There they stayed for a few days.

(John 2.12)

Even here Jesus' actions are enigmatic. Why does Jesus travel from Capernaum to Cana? For what reason does he stay there? Why only 'a few days'? The economy of John's narration (more like a chronicle than a story) again produces a plethora of gaps in the shortest space.

In the next story (John 2.13–25), Jesus travels up to Jerusalem when Passover is approaching. He goes to the Temple and discovers people selling animals, and others exchanging money. He drives them out with a whip of cords. The Jews respond by asking for a miraculous sign from Jesus, as a proof of his authority for such an action. Jesus replies with a *mashal*, a kind of riddle: 'Destroy this temple, and I will raise it again in three days' (2.19). The Jews are not unnaturally mystified. They think he is talking about the Temple buildings, which had just taken forty-six years to restore. Jesus, however, is referring to something else. He is operating at a spiritual, metaphorical level. The Temple he is alluding to, we are informed, is his body – which of course will later be destroyed but then raised after three days.

Whereas it is Jesus' actions which are enigmatic in the Cana incident (2.1–11), it is Jesus' speech which is now veiled in the Temple incident (2.13–25). Jesus' language is full of riddles and is consequently misunderstood. This is particularly visible in the next story (John 3.1–21) where Nicodemus, a ruler of the Pharisees, comes to Jesus by night to find out more about the new teacher. Here again Jesus proves evasive in his language. Now he adds *double entendre* to the use of the *mashal* or riddle. He says, 'You must be born *anothen* – again or from above' (3.3). 'The *pneuma* (which means both 'wind' and 'spirit') blows wherever it pleases'. No wonder Nicodemus finds Jesus hard to understand!

After a brief display of evasive action in 4.1–3, we see the same kind of obscure language in John 4.4–42, in Jesus' dialogue with the Samaritan woman and with his own disciples. In the first part of the story, Jesus rests by Jacob's well, near the Samaritan village of Sychar. A Samaritan woman comes to draw water, and Jesus – against the social conventions of the time – engages in conversation. 'Will you give me a drink?' he asks (4.8). After a comment of surprise from the woman, Jesus starts to talk about the 'living water' he has to offer. Since this phrase also literally means 'running water', the woman is mystified. Wells do not contain running water! Like the Jews in the Temple, and Nicodemus at night, she interprets Jesus' cryptic discourse at the literal level and becomes confused. However, unlike Nicodemus, she perseveres, and ends up imploring Jesus, 'Sir, give me this water'.

At this point, something very strange occurs. We have what appears to be another *non sequitur.* Instead of pursuing the topic of the living water, Jesus suddenly changes the subject and says, 'Go, call your husband and come back'. The South African scholar Eugene Botha has examined this statement in the light of speech act theory. He proposes that at this point Jesus breaks one of the 'cooperation principles' upon which all conversations depend. This 'cooperation principle' goes as follows: 'make your conversation contribution such as it is required, at the stage at which it occurs, by the accepted purpose or direction of the talk-exchange in which you are engaged' (Grice, cited in Stibbe 1993b: 185). One of the four maxims of this cooperation principle is the maxim of relation, 'which requires that the contribution must be relevant to the talk-exchange' (cited in Stibbe 1993b: 186). Botha's view is that Jesus flouts the maxim of relation. He likens the dialogue at this point to the following exchange: 'A says: "Don't you think Fred sometimes acts like an idiot?" To which B replies: "I planted some shrubs yesterday"' (cited in Stibbe 1993b: 188). What Botha proposes is that Jesus, up until verse 16, is engaged in a fruitless conversation. He therefore deliberately flouts the maxim of relation in order to pursue a more hopeful topic.

Botha's application of speech act theory to this dialogue is interesting. He is right to say that Jesus appears to flout the maxim of relation, but he is wrong to say that the conversation up until that moment was 'a failure', and he is equally wrong to imply that Jesus' behaviour here reveals that he is a poor conversationalist. The fact is, Jesus' language in this exchange is an example of what the literary critics call 'discontinuous dialogue' (Nuttall 1980: 128–138). Throughout the fourth gospel, Jesus employs a 'technique of deliberate transcendence' in his use of language (Nuttall 1980: 131). 'The gaps in Jesus' dialogue imply a transcending complement, a super-nature' (Nuttall 1980: 133). Nowhere is this truer than in John 4.16. Here Jesus reveals his supernatural knowledge concerning the one obstacle to the woman receiving the living water which he has to offer. That obstacle is her worship of

something other than God, namely *men*. Jesus, in his spirit, sees that
she has been married five times and is living *de facto* with a sixth. In
order for the woman to enter the life he has to offer, she must first
relinquish her idolatry of men, and then reorient herself to
worshipping God (which is why the conversation turns to 'true
worship' in 4.16f).

All this serves to underline the point being indicated at every
moment by the narrator of the fourth gospel. Jesus is an elusive
hero. He goes where God wants him to go, not where people want
him to go (John 4.1–4): he does what God wants him to do not what
people want him to do (John 2.1–11); he says what God wants him
to say, not what people want him to say (John 3.10f). The reason
for this abstruseness is given in a narratorial aside:

> Now while he was in Jerusalem at the Passover feast, many people
> saw the miraculous signs which he was doing and believed in his
> name. But Jesus would not entrust himself to them, *for he knew
> all men*. He did not need man's testimony about man, for he knew
> what was in a man [my emphasis].
>
> (John 2.23–25)

Like the Scarlet Pimpernel, Jesus is a hero who cannot trust those
around him. He is forced to be elusive in a nation where many are
on the side of darkness.

In the final story of the second section (John 4.46–54), Jesus'
abstruseness is underlined in another Cana episode. Here Jesus is
confronted by a father whose little boy is seriously ill. Jesus, once
the request is made for healing, rebukes the people around him
for depending on signs and wonders for faith. The father, however,
persists. Jesus, without explanation, heals the boy from a distance.
As in the first Cana episode (2.1–11), a request is followed by a
rebuke which is then followed, somewhat inexplicably, by a response. The gap between Jesus' rebuke and his response has to be
filled by the reader's imagination in both instances. The narrator
will not allow Jesus to lose that sense of mystery which surrounds
his words and his works.

JOHN 5–10: A READER RESPONSE

It is in the third section of the gospel that the elusiveness of Jesus
becomes most overt. This is because it is in these chapters (John
5–10) that conflict enters the story. It is from Chapter 5 onwards

that the Jewish hierarchy seeks Jesus in order to kill him. The enigmatic aspect of Jesus' characterization emerges most forcibly here because Jesus' elusiveness exists in direct proportion to the hostility that is directed against him. Since there is little if any conflict engendered by his Cana-to-Cana mission in John 2–4, there is relatively little about Jesus' actions which appears mysterious. The enigmatic and evasive features of Jesus' personality are mainly located in his use of language – discontinuous dialogue, flouting maxims, *double entendre*, the *mashal*, metaphor and so on. With the onslaught of the Jewish persecution of Jesus in John 5, all this pales into comparative insignificance. From now on, Jesus' elusiveness will increase, and this elusiveness will be located as much in his movements and actions as in his speech.

The event that precipitates this conflict is the healing miracle recorded in John 5.1–15. This narrative describes a healing which Jesus performed on the sabbath. The healed man has been crippled for 38 years and is lying on his mat by the pool of Bethesda in the Temple in Jerusalem. Jesus heads for this man – and not the many others also lying there (we are not told why) – and asks him, 'Do you want to get well?' (5.6). This is a mysterious question. Why does Jesus ask a question which surely has an obvious answer? This gap is not filled by the narrator. The motive for the question is left unexplained. The man does not even answer the question himself. The reader therefore has to guess at Jesus' intention.

The man is healed and Jesus now disappears from the scene. This sudden withdrawal from view is not an uncommon feature of Jesus' movements. We shall see it again in John 9, when Jesus disappears after healing a man born blind at another pool in Jerusalem (Siloam), again on a sabbath. In John 5.13, the Jewish authorities find the man at Bethesda and ask who healed him. The narrator explains that:

> The man who was healed had no idea who it was, for Jesus had slipped away into the crowd that was there.

In other words, the healed man is unaware *where* Jesus is and *who* Jesus is. He has no answer to give the Jews, who are angry that the healing has infringed Sabbath regulations. Later, however, Jesus finds the man in the Temple and warns him not to sin again. At this point the man goes to the Jews and informs on Jesus.

In John 5.16, the net result of this duplicity is recorded by the narrator:

So, because Jesus was doing these things on the Sabbath, the Jews persecuted him.

In verse 18, the exact nature of this persecution becomes more definite. After provoking the Jews by saying that he is only doing the Father's ongoing work (work which requires no Sabbath rest), Jesus becomes a target for assassination:

> For this reason the Jews tried all the harder to kill him; not only because he was breaking the Sabbath, but he was even calling God his own Father, making himself equal with God.

At the beginning of chapter 6, we move very abruptly from the environs of the Temple in Jerusalem to the Sea of Galilee. John 6 begins with these words:

> Some time after this, Jesus crossed to the far shore of the Sea of Galilee (that is, the Sea of Tiberias).

There is an incongruity here. The way the narrator speaks, it sounds as though we should have been on the near side of the Sea of Galilee in John 5, not in the Temple as we were. H.E. Edwards put it very well when he wrote:

> It is as if you were reading a letter from a friend in which he was telling you about salmon fishing in Scotland, and then, when you turn the page, the letter went on: 'After this I went over London Bridge'.

> (Edwards 1953: 4)

It would be easy at this point to concur with the source critics and say that the redactor has inserted John 6 rather clumsily into the present context, or that the redactor has displaced the original, logical order of events. There may be a lot of truth in this. However, such a view would miss the point which the narrator is endeavouring to make. The narrator is fully aware of the incongruity of Jesus' movements at the start of John 6. The sudden switch from the Temple to Galilee is there for a reason. It alerts the reader to a phenomenon which will recur throughout Chapters 5 to 10: the mysterious and elusive movements of the Messiah.

A few examples will need to suffice: first of all, we should note the way in which Jesus withdraws from the crowds after the feeding of the 5,000 in John 6.15. He knows they want to make him a king. He therefore slips away and conceals himself. This quiet disappearance will be a frequent occurrence from now on.

Then, in John 6.16–21, the narrator tells of an incident in which the disciples are out on a rough sea at night. All of a sudden, Jesus appears walking on the water to calm their nerves with the words, 'It is I; don't be afraid'. They take Jesus on to the boat and immediately they reach the shore. Here again Jesus' movements are mysterious. He suddenly appears from nowhere, walking on the sea. Just as suddenly, once he is on board, the disciples reach their destination. It goes without saying that this is elusive behaviour. It is the conduct of a man who can transcend the laws of gravity and defy the limitations of time and space. No wonder scholars have seen this story as a misplaced resurrection appearance!

The day after this episode, a crowd goes searching for Jesus in boats. They find him on the other side of the Sea of Galilee. They ask him, 'Rabbi, when did you get here?' (6.25). This is a third example of Jesus' mystifying movements. The crowds seek after Jesus (6.24, *zetein*) but he is always one step ahead of them, and never where they expect.

In Chapter 7, we have the very strange behaviour of Jesus described in the first episode (7.1–13). At the time of the Feast of Tabernacles, the brothers of Jesus try to persuade him to go to Judea to perform some miracles there. Jesus replies with an emphatic no. 'The right time for me has not yet come; for you any time is right', he says (7.7). However, after his brothers have left for Judea, Jesus goes anyway, but waits until half way through the Feast. He goes *en krupto*, 'in secret', not *parresia*, or 'openly' (7.10, an adverb used nine times in John). Truly Jesus is an enigmatic character. He will not conform to human pressure; he operates according to a very different timetable.

In the rest of John 7, we see the first of a number of 'great escapes' by Jesus. These start in verse 30:

7.30: At this they tried to seize him, but no one laid a hand on him, because his time had not yet come.

7.44: Some wanted to seize him, but no one laid a hand on him.

8.59: At this they picked up stones to stone him, but Jesus hid himself, slipping away from the Temple grounds.

10.39: Again they tried to seize him, but he escaped their grasp.

It is in these chapters (7–10) that the enmity of the Jewish authorities reaches fever pitch. They become hell bent upon seizing Jesus (*piazein*, to arrest, is the common verb). But he escapes their grasp every time (*oudeis exebalen ep' auton ten cheira*: no one laid their hands on him).

If we put all these examples of evasive movements in John 5–10 together, what emerges are the following kinds of elusiveness on the part of Jesus the Messiah:

1 Unexplained withdrawals from the story (5.13; 9.12).
2 Mysterious escapes from places of hostility (8.59).
3 Mysterious elusiveness within places of hostility (7.30; 7.44; 10.39).
4 Elusive behaviour towards people with wrong motives (6.15; 6.22–26).
5 Mysterious appearances (6.19).
6 Quiet reappearances in the story (5.14; 9.35).
7 Movement which seems to transcend time and space (6.1; 6.20–21).
8 Secret journeys (7.10).

Put all these together, and the reader cannot help but feel that the hero of the fourth gospel has become a kind of Johannine Pimpernel: 'They seek him here, they seek him there, those Jews they seek him everywhere!'

What reinforces this impression is the fact that this elusiveness is not only suggested by the movements of Jesus. It is also suggested by the language of Jesus. As we would expect in a story in the ancient Hebrew tradition, the elusive character of Jesus is indicated, in the main, by action and by speech.

As far as speech is concerned, notice in particular the use of the *mashal* or the riddle. When confronted by the divided crowds in Jerusalem, Jesus utters a very strange saying:

> I am with you for only a short time, and then I go to the one who sent me. You will look for me, but you will not find me; and where I am, you cannot come.
>
> (John 7.34: see also 8.21)

The place where Jesus is going is heaven, where he will enjoy once again the glory which he shared with the Father before the world was made. The crowd, however, interprets the riddle incorrectly – at a literal level:

> Where does this man intend to go that we cannot find him? Will he go where our people live scattered among the Greeks?
>
> (John 7.35)

The *mashal* is too much for the crowds. They do not understand about Jesus' eternal origins or his eternal destiny (7.41–42). Consequently, Jesus' language is beyond them.

If the *mashal* is an indication of the abstruseness of Jesus' language, so is the *paroimia*. This word is used by the narrator just after the opening of the Good Shepherd discourse in John 10 (see 10.6). The NIV translates it as a 'figure of speech'. A better translation would be a 'cryptic word-picture'. Jesus' language about shepherds and sheep is an indirect commentary on the failure of the Jewish leaders to behave as true pastors of the people of Israel. Again, this is an example of veiled speech.

Perhaps the most revealing moment in these chapters – as far as the characterization of Jesus is concerned – is after the lengthy dialogue in John 6.25–59. Just after Jesus has preached his homily on 'Manna from heaven' in the Capernaum synagogue (6.59), many of his disciples say, 'This is a hard teaching. Who can accept it?' The phrase translated 'hard teaching' is *skleros logos*. It is a phrase which functions as a perfect title for Jesus who, in the prologue of John's gospel, is called God's *Logos*. In John 5–10, Jesus is truly the *Skleros Logos*, the Difficult Word. He is difficult in both his movements and his language. He is not an easy person to grasp, either at the level of comprehension or at the level of apprehension. But then the reader was warned, in John 1.5, that the light shines in the darkness, but the darkness cannot grasp it. The reader was warned that Jesus is the elusive Christ.

JOHN 11–12: A READER RESPONSE

In the final section of Part 1 of the gospel (chapters 1 to 12), Jesus raises Lazarus from the dead (11.1–44), a miracle which finally seals his fate with the Jewish authorities (11.45–53). Jesus withdraws for a while, much to the consternation of those who are looking for him (11.54–56). Jesus then returns to Bethany, Lazarus' home, and is anointed (12.1–11) prior to his entry into Jerusalem on a donkey (12.12–19). The section ends with several speeches by Jesus and a summary by the narrator (12.20–36, 37–43, 44–50).

The elusiveness of Jesus is again confirmed at a number of points. He continues to use cryptic speech (11.9–10; 11.25–26; 12.24), and his actions prove elusive as well (11.54; 12.16; 12.36). Perhaps most enigmatic of all is his delay in returning to heal Lazarus. There are a number of reasons for this, but the most relevant for our purposes is Jesus' refusal to act under pressure from others. For human beings, any time is right (7.6). But for the elusive Messiah, responses to requests are made according to divine intuition, to the leadings of the Spirit. His delay must therefore be interpreted in the light of his abstruseness.

JOHN 13–17: A READER RESPONSE

I have called Part 2 of the gospel, 'The Departure of Jesus'. The beginning of John 13 signals this note of imminent return to the Father:

> It was just before the Passover Feast. Jesus knew that the time had come for him to leave this world and go to the Father.
>
> (John 13.1)

Here too the Messiah is portrayed as an elusive Revealer.

The farewell (John 13–17) begins with an enigmatic action (13.1–30). Jesus gets down from his seat at the last supper, undresses, wraps a towel around his waist, washes his disciples' feet and then returns to his seat at the head of the table. These actions are highly symbolic. The descent from the table symbolizes Jesus' descent from heaven. His removal of his outer clothes symbolizes his humility in becoming incarnate as a human being. His washing of the disciples' feet symbolizes the atoning death he will die on the cross – a death which will wash his disciples of their sins. His return to the table symbolizes his return to the Father in heaven. The whole scene is carefully choreographed to represent the overall shape and purpose of his descent to earth and ascent to heaven, as is suggested by his laying down of his clothes in 13.4 (*tithemi*, the same verb which is used for the laying down of his life in 10.11, 15, 17) and his taking up of the same garments in 13.12 (*lambano*, the same verb which is used for the taking up of his life in 10.17 and 18). For the perceptive reader, Jesus' clothes (*himatia*, 13.4) function as a clue to the symbolism of Jesus' elusive action (see the *himatia* which Jesus is forced to discard at the cross, 19.23).

So the farewell begins with an elusive action. Enigmatic speech is not lacking either. Peter fails to comprehend Jesus in 13.31–38 ('Where I am going, you cannot come', the same *mashal* as in 7.34); Thomas fails to understand Jesus' metaphor of the way in 14.1–7; Philip fails to understand the nature of Jesus' revelation in 14.8–14. In fact, throughout the farewell discourses, the disciples find Jesus' words *skleros logos*, 'hard teaching'. It is not until 16.29 that they exclaim, 'Now you are speaking clearly and without figures of speech'. Here the vocabulary is very revealing. The word translated 'clearly' is *parresia*, the same word which is used in 7.4 where the brothers of Jesus encourage him to move about 'openly'. This creates a telling unity between the action and the speech of John's hero. Neither are conducted *parresia*, 'plainly' or 'openly'.

Two further features support the sense of Jesus' abstruseness in the farewell discourses. First of all we cannot neglect the famous *crux interpretum* at 14.31, where Jesus says 'Come now; let us leave', and then proceeds to give three more chapters of (mostly) monologue. Source critics use this apparent aporia to highlight the different hands involved in the composition of the gospel. The common explanation is that a later hand has clumsily inserted Chapters 15–17 after Chapter 14 and before Chapter 18. This seems to be confirmed by the logic of following 14.31 with 18.1:

'Come now; let us leave' (14.31).

Jesus left with his disciples and crossed the Kidron valley.
                  (18.1, omitting the redactional phrase, *tauta eipon*)

Source critics contend that the smooth flow from 14.31 to 18.1 supports their view that a final redactor added new material to the farewell.

This is a plausible suggestion. However, let us suppose for a moment that the redactor was well aware of the apparent tension between 'Come now; let us leave', and the speech material which followed. Let us suppose for a moment that he was not a literary buffoon and that he saw some purpose here. What might that purpose be? The most obvious answer is that he did not remove Jesus' exhortation to leave because he saw it as consonant with the overarching theme of Jesus' elusiveness. The redactor allowed the exhortation to stay because he wanted to keep Jesus 'on the move' at a time when 'the prince of this world' (the devil) was approaching (14.30). Having Jesus remain in one place on the evening of his arrest and the night before his death would have been dissonant with Jesus' elusiveness. So the redactor allows Jesus to move to an unspecified location in order to heighten the suspense over Jesus' imminent capture. This, I propose, was all the more necessary at a time when there was much to be said to the disciples concerning the future.

The second observation concerns another famous *crux inter-pretum*. This one involves Jesus' statement in 16.5:

> Now I am going to him who sent me, yet none of you asks me, 'Where are you going?'

Source critics often point out that this is illogical. In John 13.36, Peter asks Jesus, 'Where are you going?' So Jesus is wrong to say in 16.5 that none of the disciples ask the question. This inconsistency further supports the thesis that John 15–17 was added by a clumsy redactor, who failed to see that the statement of Jesus in 16.5 no longer applied.

Again, there is sense in this argument. However, let us again suppose that the redactor was not illiterate in the ways of story-telling. Let us suppose he allowed the statement to remain because he saw it as a challenging 'gap'. What might this gap be?

One possible solution is that Jesus is being deliberately abstruse again, and that this serves to bring out aspects of the disciples' character. I will quote the interpretation which I offered in my narrative-critical commentary on John:

> A sequential reading reveals something of the importance of Jesus' question in 16.5 for the characterization of the disciples. The reader knows that a proper response to Jesus' 'Now I am going to him who sent me' (16.5a) is the question, 'Where are you going?' asked by Peter in 13.36 and by Thomas (less overtly) in 14.5. The silence of the disciples at this point reveals their caution. When Peter asked this question before, it led to a severe warning: 'I tell you the truth, before the cock crows, you will disown me three times!' (13.38). When Thomas asked this question in 14.5, it led to a thinly veiled rebuke: 'If you really knew me, you would know my Father as well'. The silence of the disciples in Jn 16.5 is therefore entirely explicable. The disciples have become very cautious about asking questions. In spite of the constant invitations by Jesus to ask things of both himself and the Father (14.13–14, for example), the paradox is that every time a disciple asks a question in John 13.31–14.31 it is greeted less than enthusiastically by Jesus.
>
> (Stibbe 1993a: 172)

Viewed in this light, the statement of Jesus in John 16.5 is seen to make at least some possible sense, and to highlight something of how recondite Jesus really is!

JOHN 18–19: A READER RESPONSE

With the arrival of Chapter 18, the situation changes. John 18 begins in the garden across the Kidron valley where Jesus regularly met with his disciples (18.2). We do not know eactly where this garden was, nor to whom it belonged. The narrator is not interested in specifying such details. The main point of interest is the fact that this garden was a favourite meeting place and that Jesus deliberately chose to go there, knowing full well that this would be the first place to which Judas would lead the arresting party. This is indeed what occurs (18.3) and Jesus is captured and led away.

The reader should not miss the point concerning the garden. The narrator wants us to realize that the elusive Christ knows that he will be captured, and that he voluntarily offers himself to those who have been seeking him throughout the gospel. That is why, when the soldiers arrive, Jesus goes out from the garden and asks (twice): 'Who is it you want?' (18.4, 7). The verb used here is *zeteo* ('I seek') which we have already noted is a favourite thematic word, linked to the presentation of Jesus as an elusive hero. At the moment when Jesus says, 'I am he' (i.e. 'I am the one you want'), the narrator records that 'they [the soldiers] drew back and fell to the ground' (18.6). Nearly all the commentators interpret this as a response of awe at Jesus' revelatory use of the divine name, 'I AM!' This, they say, is the standard response to a theophany. But surely there is another reason. Is this reaction not one of amazement? That after all their seeking, the Jews finally find the elusive Messiah?

For the rest of the passion narrative, Jesus is bound and led to Annas, then to Pilate, then to Golgotha. Consequently, his abstruseness from this point on is located entirely in his speech. In fact, the classic instance of Jesus' linguistic evasiveness is in these chapters, in Jesus' interrogation by Pilate from 18.28–19.16a. Here Jesus employs the device of 'discontinuous dialogue' with considerable skill. As A.D. Nuttall puts it:

> When Jesus is asked if he is the king of the Jews, he answers neither yes or no but instead asks a question of his own. When he is asked what he has done, he answers not that question but the earlier one with the mysterious, 'My kingdom is not of this world'. Even so, he skips one logical stage: to make the logic fully explicit he would presumably have had to say something like, 'I am a king, yes, but not of the Jews nor of anything earthly'. This logical ellipse seems to trouble Pilate and he asks, seeking

confirmation, 'Art thou a king, then?' and hears in answer the words, 'Thou sayest I am'.

(Nuttall 1980: 129)

Jesus' aloofness before Pilate seals his fate. His failure to provide an adequate defence secures his *pathos* (scene of extreme suffering), and he is led away to be crucified outside the walls of Jerusalem.

JOHN 20–21: A READER RESPONSE

With the resurrection, we might expect an end to the elusiveness of Jesus. But this is not so. The resurrection narratives begin with the question, 'Where is Jesus' body?' (20.1–10). When the risen Jesus does appear, he is not recognized by Mary Magdalene; she thinks, at first, that he is the gardener (20.11–18). When she does recognize Jesus, he tells her not to hold on to him (20.17). The risen Jesus must be allowed to retain his elusiveness; the sacred still cannot be grasped.

Immediately afterwards, Jesus passes through locked doors to address the disciples (20.19–23). Thomas is not present, so he is permitted a personal encounter in 20.24–29. In the final chapter (John 21), Jesus appears at the lakeside but again is not recognized to begin with. He then spends time restoring Peter, but does so with yet another *mashal* indicating the kind of martyrdom which Peter will have to face in the future:

> 'I tell you the truth, when you were younger you dressed yourself and went where you wanted; but when you are old you will stretch out your hands, and someone else will dress you and lead you where you do not want to go'.

(John 21.18)

The story then concludes with a comment by the narrator:

> Jesus did many other things as well. If every one of them were written down, I suppose that even the whole world would not have room for the books that would be written.

Here we are presented with a final tribute to the mystery of Jesus. This hero, says the narrator, is altogether too inexhaustible to be contained by a book or by a library of books. He is quintessentially the elusive Christ.

Looking at John 20–21 as a whole, one theme is brought to the fore which we have not yet observed. This is the theme of recognition. Because Jesus is portrayed as an elusive Messiah, the great challenge of the gospel is to recognize who he really is. As the narrator says in 1.10: 'He was in the world, and though the world was made through him, the world did not *recognize* him' [my emphasis]. Consequently, what Aristotle called *anagnorisis* ('recognizing the hero') is a gauntlet thrown down to every character who meets Jesus. As Culpepper has said,

> Plot development in John . . . is a matter of how Jesus' identity comes to be recognized and how it fails to be recognized. Not only is Jesus' identity progressively revealed by the repetitive signs and discourses and the progressive enhancement of metaphorical and symbolic images, but each episode has essentially the same plot as the story as a whole. Will Nicodemus, the Samaritan woman, or the lame man recognize Jesus and thereby receive eternal life? The story is repeated over and over. No one can miss it.
>
> (Culpepper 1983: 88–89)

In John 20–21, the same challenge is given to a different group of characters – to Peter, the beloved disciple, Mary Magdalene, Thomas, and the rest. This time they must recognize the risen Jesus. Even here, with his own disciples, Jesus is elusive!

CONCLUSION

Looking at the gospel as a whole, our reader response criticism has revealed a hero who cannot easily be grasped. When it comes to understanding Jesus, the narrator constantly leaves us with logical ellipses or gaps which we, the reader, must try to fill in. The one telling the story is therefore an elusive narrator, just as the one about whom the narrator is speaking is an elusive hero. In this respect, the 'teller' and the 'told' compliment one another perfectly.

As far as Jesus himself is concerned, his abstruseness is indicated by his speech and by his actions. In Chapters 2–4, this dimension of his character is suggested mainly by his language. In Chapters 5–10, it is suggested mainly by his actions. In John 11–12 it is mainly by action, and 13–17 it is mainly by speech. In John 18–19 it is suggested mainly by speech, and in 20–21, mainly by action. In true

Hebrew style, John therefore relies very heavily upon the words and the deeds of his hero to create a sense of character.

But why does John do this? Why does he portray Jesus as a kind of first century 'Scarlet Pimpernel'? There are a number of answers (see Stibbe 1991: 29–37). One has to do with John's theology. If Jesus is one with God (10.30), then he must be seen to have some of the same characteristics as Yahweh in the Old Testament. Yahweh is portrayed as a deity who is elusive. He is *absconditus atque praesans*, hidden but at the same time present. That is why Isaiah declares, 'Truly you are a God who hides himself' (Isaiah 45.15). It is very possible that John saw God in terms of 'Elusive Presence' and sought to instill the same qualities in the character of Jesus.

But more important is the intended effect which this elusiveness has on the reader. John portrays Jesus with an intentional obscurity because it acts as a source of hermeneutical seduction, tantalizing and drawing the reader back to the story in order to 'seek' the hero once again. Every time this happens, the game of hide-and-seek is now played out in the life of the reader, but to the readers who persevere in their search, eternal life is the great reward.

Chapter 2

Plot

The first book I ever read about history was R.G. Collingwood's classic, *The Idea of History*, first published in 1946 (see Collingwood 1953). I was immediately impressed by his critique of what he called 'the common-sense theory' of history-writing. This is the popularly held notion that a truthful historical account is one in which the historian merely reproduces the ready-made statements of his authorities (Collingwood 1953: 234–5). These 'ready-made statements' are understood by common-sense historians as sacred and authoritative texts which must not be tampered with in any way. As Collingwood wrote, 'He must not mutilate them; he must not add to them; and, above all, he must not contradict them in any way' (p.235). 'For him . . . what his authorities tell him is the truth, the whole accessible truth, and nothing but the truth' (p.235). For the historian, history-writing is simply a matter of reproducing what is recorded in various authorities. Like the landscape painter who thinks that s/he is reproducing the actual shapes and colours of nature, the common-sense historian believes that s/he is producing a copy of life as it really has been lived.

Collingwood repudiates this 'common-sense' view. It is, in reality, nonsense rather than common sense. Every historian selects from his sources the material which s/he thinks is important. S/he interpolates in them things which they do not explicitly say. S/he even criticizes them by amending what is regarded as wrong (p.235). However hard the historian tries, s/he cannot help selecting, simplifying, schematizing, omitting and adding in the process of historical construction (p.236). The reason for this is because history-writing is not a purely objective science. It is a discipline requiring what Collingwood calls 'the historical imagination', the faculty through which events are synthesized into a coherent story.

From this basis, Collingwood proceeds to draw comparisons between the way in which the historian and the novelist create their narrative worlds. Like the novelist, the historian seeks to reveal characters acting in a consistent way. Like the novelist, the historian also wants to describe incidents developing in a manner determined by what Collingwood calls 'a necessity internal to themselves' (p.242). Collingwood refines the analogy between the novelist and the historian in this way:

> Each of them makes it his business to construct a picture which is partly a narrative of events, partly a description of situations, exhibition of motives, analysis of characters. Each aims at making his picture a coherent whole, where every character and every situation is so bound up with the rest that this character and this situation cannot but act in this way, and we cannot imagine him as acting otherwise. The novel and the history must both of them make sense.
>
> (Collingwood 1953: 245)

So there are similarities between the novelist and the historian. The major difference, of course, is that 'the historian's picture is meant to be true' (p.246). 'The historian's picture stands in a peculiar relation to something called evidence' (p.246).

THE PLOT OF THE FOURTH GOSPEL

This is all relevant to our study of John's gospel. Most conservative readers of the fourth gospel are apt to employ a common-sense theory of John's history-writing. In other words, they assume that John has accurately and faithfully recorded the sayings, actions and events contained in his authoritative sources. This view is cherished with particular possessiveness by fundamentalist Christians. But readers who take this line rarely stop to think carefully about the problems inherent in such an assumption. If the synoptic gospels are John's authoritative sources, then he has exercised extraordinary freedom in reinterpreting them. If other sources were at John's disposal, then it needs to be conceded that we can only guess what they might have been. Even if we decide to affirm that John used distinctive sources – ones independent from the Synoptics – then it would still have to be admitted that he has produced an *interpretation* of those sources. So either way, the common-sense view is difficult to sustain.

A much more plausible thesis is that John used his 'historical imagination' in the reconstruction of Jesus' history. In respect to character, he created out of his sources a hero with consistent features. These consistent features I have summed up, in chapter 1, with the word 'elusiveness'. That the historical Jesus was himself an elusive figure is very likely. It is interesting to note that Gerd Theissen, in a recent narrative reconstruction of the life of the historical Jesus, stresses this very characteristic. In his study, *The Shadow of the Galilean,* Jesus is depicted as a shadowy figure, a man whose radicalism meant that he was constantly on the move: 'He appeared in some places unexpectedly and then soon disappeared again' (Theissen 1987: 119). So the elusiveness of Jesus in John's gospel is not an invention *de novo.* It is an interpretation of features witnessed in Jesus' own life. What John does, using the suggestion of elusiveness in his sources, is to turn it into the primary character trait of Jesus – the character trait which gives meaning to his hero's words and actions at every point.

What is true of John's characterization of Jesus is equally true of John's creation of a plot for his gospel. By plot is meant the organization of events into a coherent unity characterized by a causal and temporal logic. Historians, when they reconstruct history, form events into a story with a plot. As Hayden White puts it:

> In the process of studying a given complex of events, he [the historian] begins to perceive the possible story form that such events may figure. In his narrative account of how this set of events took on the shape he perceives to inhere within it, he emplots his account as a story of a particular kind.
>
> (White 1978: 49)

What White is saying here is that a historian reconstructing the past will not always record a series of events in the order in which they originally occurred. That would result in the pure form of history known as the chronicle. Instead, the historian arranges events into a sequence with a beginning, a middle and an end (i.e. a plot). History-writing therefore involves arranging events in a story with formal coherence.

In the case of the fourth gospel, John arranges his historical material into a story with a plot. All four evangelists had to select and then arrange the various data from their sources into a meaningful whole. John is no exception. Indeed, Culpepper argues that 'Conscious plotting of the narrative is more obvious in John than in the Synoptics, even if its structure is no tighter than theirs' (1983: 86). As evidence for John's conscious plotting of material, we may point to three factors: the causal, temporal and structural nature of John's organization of events. We wil look at each of these three features in turn.

THE CAUSAL ASPECT OF JOHN'S PLOT

As far as causality is concerned, some comments by Horace about tragedy will form a helpful backcloth:

> In an ideal tragedy we look for a true beginning . . ., a true central point, and a true consummation or end. Towards the central point the whole action must ascend in orderly sequence, and from it descend in an equally ordered sequence to the end.
>
> (cited in Hitchcock 1923: 16)

Accordingly, there are five acts or stages in a tragic story. As Hitchcock summarizes it in his essay, 'Is the Fourth Gospel a Drama?':

> There is the beginning, the development towards the central point, the central point, the development towards the end, the end.
>
> (Hitchcock 1923: 16)

Although John is not a tragedy, this Horatian framework does help us to see something of the causality of the plot of the fourth gospel. After a dramatic prologue and introduction (John 1), the gospel story is established in 'the beginning'. This first stage is described in John 2–4, where Jesus begins his public ministry with a journey from Cana in Galilee (2.1–11), to Jerusalem, through Samaria and then back to Cana again (4.45–54). Here the character and mission of Jesus is firmly established in the mind of the reader.

The second stage of the plot is 'the development towards the central point'. This is John 5–10, where conflict begins to emerge. Here the *theomachus* or 'enemy of God' comes to the fore, in the form of the Jewish hierarchy in Jerusalem. They plot to kill Jesus from 5.19 onwards, and make every attempt to seize or to stone him as Jesus performs his charismatic ministry of teaching and healing.

The third stage of the plot is described in John 11–12. This is the central point in the story, both thematically and mathematically. The raising of Lazarus is the seventh miracle performed by Jesus in the gospel. The previous six are:

1 the transformation of water into wine (2.1–11);
2 the healing of the official's son (4.45–54);
3 the healing of the man at Bethesda (5.1–15);
4 the multiplication of the loaves (6.1–15);
5 the miraculous crossing of the sea (6.16–21);
6 the healing of the man born blind (9.1–41).

Since seven is the perfect number in Judaism, the raising of Lazarus in 11.1–44 needs to be seen as the climactic miracle. Indeed, it is the most dramatic, lengthy and provocative of all the miracles. It is this event which precipitates Jesus' downfall (11.45–53). It is from this point that the Sanhedrin '*plotted* to take his life' (11.53) [my emphasis].

The fourth stage of the plot is the development towards the end. This is described in John 13–19, where Jesus bids farewell to his followers and is crucified. These seven chapters of narrative cover the last twenty-four hours of Jesus' life, from Thursday evening to Friday evening in Passover week. Here Jesus prepares for and experiences the fate which the Sanhedrin have planned for him in stage three.

The fifth and final stage of the plot is John 20, the resurrection of Jesus. This is the 'end' of the story, with John 21 functioning as an epilogue. It is here that the disciples meet the risen Jesus, and it is here that the climactic *anagnorisis* or recognition scene occurs. This takes place when Thomas looks at the risen Jesus and says, 'My Lord and my God' (20.28). This Christological confession forms the climactic denouement in the plot of the gospel.

THE TEMPORAL ASPECT OF JOHN'S PLOT

Seen in this light, there is a clear sense of causality in the plot of the fourth gospel. There is also a clear sense of temporality. Aristotle spoke of the need for a beginning, a middle and an end in the temporal unity of a story. This is what we find in John's gospel. The events of the story are given temporal unity by the threefold mention of Passover. Passover is the Jewish festival which commemorates the exodus of the Israelites from slavery in Egypt (see Exodus 12). It occurs once every year in the spring. In John's gospel, three such festivals are mentioned:

2.13: When it was almost time for the Jewish Passover, Jesus went up to Jerusalem.

6.4: The Jewish Passover Feast was near.

13.1: It was just before the Passover Feast.

These three feasts are important for our appreciation of the story time in the gospel's plot. There is obviously a period of one year between John 2 and John 6, and a period of another year between John 6 and John 13. In Chapters 13 to 17, the narrator locates us 'just before the Passover Feast' (13.1) and in Chapters 18–19 on the Day of Preparation (19.14, 31, 42) – in other words, the day before Passover when the lambs were slaughtered by the priests in the Temple courts. Chapters 13–19 therefore cover a period of twenty-four hours. Add Chapters 20–21, and John 13–21 can be said to cover a period of under two weeks. This is in marked contrast to the story time of John 1–12, which covers a period of over two years. Clearly the speed of the story slows down dramatically in Part 2 of the gospel.

Something of this deceleration is visible in the way in which John 11–12 prepares for the rest of the gospel. Here the narrator keeps emphasizing the inexorable progress of time towards the third and fateful Passover. In 11.55, the narrator tells us that 'it was almost time for the Jewish Passover'. In 12.1, we are told that it is now 'six days before the Passover'. In 12.12, the narrator uses the phrase 'the next day' to keep the suspense alive. Then, finally, in 13.1 we are informed that 'it was just before the Passover Feast' and that 'Jesus knew that the time had come'.

This last quotation is very significant. In the phrase 'the time had come' the narrator uses the word *hora*, translated 'time' in the NIV but literally meaning 'hour'. The hour of Jesus is the divinely appointed time-limit within which Jesus must have completed the work which his Father had given him to do. This word is used on a number of occasions in John 1–12 to remind the reader that there is a temporal horizon which functions as the goal of Jesus' work:

2.4: 'Dear woman, why do you involve me? My time [*hora*] has not yet come'.

7.30: At this they tried to seize him, but no one laid a hand on him because his time [*hora*] had not yet come.

8.20: Yet no one seized him, because his time [*hora*] had not yet come.

With the third Passover, the promised 'hour' arrives. The narrator can say, 'The time [*hora*] had come for Jesus to leave this world and return to the Father' (13.1).

As far as causality and temporality is concerned, the gospel contains a discernible order, direction and teleology in its plot. Seen as a whole, John's story contains a kind of *Passover plot* in which events follow one another with inexorable logic towards that climactic hour in which Jesus is crucified at precisely the moment when the Passover lambs were being slaughtered in the Temple.

THE STRUCTURAL ASPECT OF JOHN'S PLOT

We have looked at the causal and temporal aspects of John's plotting of events. We now turn to the structural dimension of the same. For this we will need to use the insights of structuralism, an ideology committed to exposing deep structures in all aspects of life.

In *John as Storyteller* I have described how structuralist approaches to biblical narrative have gone in three recognizable directions (1992: 34–39). The first of these, deriving from Claude Lévi-Strauss, is the *binary* approach. This approach consists of exposing the binary oppositions in biblical stories, and the degree to which they are mediated. The second direction, deriving from Vladimir Propp, is the *functional* approach. This approach consists of a general description of the plot functions in a biblical story, followed by a comparison with other stories which share the same deep structure. The third direction (and the most recent in time), derives from A.J. Greimas. This is commonly referred to as *actantial* analysis (i.e. analysis of actants or characters). In this approach, exegesis consists of mapping a given biblical story against Greimas' universal structure of narrative possibilities. It is this third approach which is most helpful for exposing the structural character of John's plot.

Summaries of Greimas' model of narrative are widespread so we can be brief. Essentially his argument is this: that all stories can be reduced to a deep narrative structure, a kind of transcultural and universal grammar of storytelling. In diagrammatical form, Greimas' structure looks like this:

SENDER	Object	RECEIVER
	axis of communication	
	axis of volition	
	axis of power	
OPPONENT	Subject	HELPER

This deep structure has three axes: an axis of communication, an axis of volition and an axis of power. These three axes are basic plot functions. The axis of communication is the commission; someone tells someone else to undertake a task. The axis of volition is the quest; the hero undertakes to do a particular work, to fulfil a particular mission. The axis of power is the conflict experienced by this quester.

These three axes have four character-types or *actants* associated with them. The first is the Sender (sometimes called the Originator). S/he gives a commission to a second actant, the Receiver. The Receiver in turn comes into conflict with the third actant, the Opponent. However, s/he receives assistance from the fourth actant, the Helper. Throughout all of this, the Receiver is involved in a quest. This receiver is the Subject and the quest itself is the Object.

In order to see how this structure actually works, let us invent a story. This story concerns a professor of biblical studies who asks a lecturer in her department to do a project for her. The project involves going to Jerusalem to find what she believes are the skeletal remains of the apostle James. The lecturer willingly agrees (as good lecturers always do) and sets forth on his journey. On arrival, he starts making enquiries in various quarters in the city of Jerusalem. He befriends a Palestinian woman who helps him from place to place. However, dark forces are also at work. An anti-Christian terrorist group called the Middle Eastern Front (MEF) gets wind of the fact that the lecturer is close to an important archaeological find. This is deemed to be of political significance. Members of the organization therefore make an attempt on the lecturer's life. However, at the critical moment, his Palestinian girlfriend throws herself in the way of the bullet, using her body as a shield, and she is killed instead. Desperately grieved, the lecturer vows to fulfil his task so that her death is not in vain. Now with the help of police protection he organizes a dig, finds some remains, which are later identified as those of a first century man who was almost certainly stoned to death. The professor flies out and is delighted.

If we chart this story against Greimas' grid we can see that the Sender is the professor and the Receiver is the lecturer. The axis of communication is the task which the professor gives to the lecturer. The Opponent in the story is the Middle Eastern Front. The Helper is the lecturer's Palestinian girlfriend and the police. The axis of power is the conflict which the lecturer experiences in the undertaking of what he thought would be a purely academic task. The Subject of the story is of course the lecturer and the Object is the supposed remains of the Apostle James. This is the axis of volition and constitutes the quest of the story. Overall, my rather unoriginal fiction looks like this:

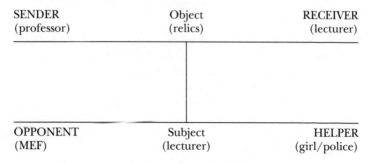

SENDER (professor)	Object (relics)	RECEIVER (lecturer)
OPPONENT (MEF)	Subject (lecturer)	HELPER (girl/police)

This example, in very simple terms, give us an idea of how Greimas' model of structuralist literary criticism actually works.

A STRUCTURAL ANALYSIS OF JOHN'S PLOT

When we apply this kind of actantial model to the plot of John's plot, we begin to see its usefulness. Clearly there is a Sender figure in the plot of the fourth gospel. Indeed, the very label 'Sender' seems tailor-made for an actantial approach to John because the verb 'send' is used ubiquitously throughout the gospel. *Pempein* is used thirty-two times and *apostellein* twenty-eight times. It is God the Father who is most often the subject of these verbs; indeed John characterizes God as 'the Sending Father'.

The Receiver of this 'sending' is Jesus, the hero of the story. That Jesus is the Receiver of the Father's commission is indicated by Jesus' repeated description of his Father as 'the one who sent me'. On twenty-four occasions, *pempein* is used in the phrase *ho pempsas me* (the one who sent me) and on seventeen occasions *apostellein* is used of the sending of Jesus by the Father. In depicting Jesus as 'the one sent', John is presenting Jesus in theological terms as the focus of an emissary Christology, and in narrative terms as the Receiver of the Sender's commission.

What is the commission which the Father gives to Jesus? The answer is an *ergon*, a work or a task. Though there is no scene in which this *ergon* is explicitly described, Jesus does speak of 'the very work which the Father has given me to finish' (John 5.36). In the plot of the gospel there is a prescribed time-limit (designated and anticipated by the concept of the hour of Jesus) by which this work must have been completed. Jesus' cry on the cross, 'it is finished', reveals that Calvary marks the completion of Jesus' mission and the fulfilment of the divinely commissioned task. At this point, the cross becomes the place from which Jesus, as it were, can 'return to sender'.

The axis of communication therefore consists of a commission given by the Sending Father to the Receiving Son. The object of this commission is the work given by the Father for Jesus to do. There is no text in the fourth gospel in which this commission is actually given. It is presupposed throughout. However, this does not mean that communication between the Father and the Son does not happen. Far from it: the axis or channel of communication between the Sender and Receiver is kept open throughout the narrative. Sometimes this is suggested to the reader by various statements of Jesus, for example:

'The Son can do nothing by himself; he can do only what he sees his Father doing' (5.19)

'By myself I can do nothing; I judge only as I hear' (5.30)

At other times it is suggested to the reader by the prayers directed by the Son to the Father:

'Father, I thank you that you have heard me. I knew that you always hear me' (11.41–2)

'Father, glorify your name!' (12.28)

'Father, the time has come' (17.1)

These observations help us to map the first aspect of John's plot against Greimas' actantial structure as follows:

SENDER	Object	RECEIVER
(Father)	(work)	(Jesus)

axis of communication

If we move now to the axis of volition, we are faced with the issue of the quest in John's story. Who is the Subject of this quest? What is the Object of the quest? If we look at what is arguably the central plot statement of the gospel, John 3.16, we note that the Subject of the quest is Jesus, and the Object is to bring life to those who believe in him. 'God so loved the world that he gave his one and only Son, *that whoever believes in him shall not perish but have eternal life'* [my emphasis]. This means that we can be more specific about the *ergon* which the Father gives to Jesus. The *ergon* is to give *zoe*, 'life', to the children of God. A number of factors confirm this; first, the prologue, where the narrator says of Jesus, 'in him was life' (v.3); secondly, the prevalence of the noun *zoe* in John (thirty-six times, sixteen times in the Synoptics); thirdly, Jesus' description of his quest: 'I have come that they may have life, and have it to the full' (10.10); fourthly, the narrator's declaration of his purpose in writing the story in John 20.31. 'These things are written . . . that you may have life in his name'.

We can therefore fill in the second axis, the axis of volition, as follows:

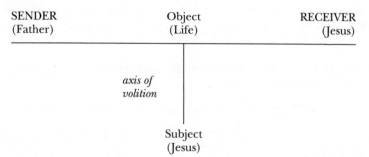

SENDER	Object	RECEIVER
(Father)	(Life)	(Jesus)

axis of volition

Subject
(Jesus)

Using the word 'volition' literally, we can see that this axis consists of Jesus doing 'the will' of the one who sent him (4.34).

This still leaves one of the axes, the axis of power. In the development of the plot in John's story we are not really aware of conflict until Chapter 5. From this moment onwards, various characters are depicted as the opponents of Jesus, as those resisting his desire to fulfil his quest. These figures fulfil the role of the *theomachus*, the enemies of God; they are principally the Jews, the Pharisees, the chief priests, Caiaphas, Judas, Annas, the world and, of course, the devil. All these, at one time or another, try to stand against Jesus in the fulfilling of his mission. They occupy the Opponent pole of the axis of power.

All this leaves the Helper figure. Who fulfils this plot function in John's story? Here we confront a very interesting problem. Can it really be said that anyone is a consistent Helper to Jesus in the fulfilling of his quest? Is there anyone who helps Jesus to go to the cross in order to give life to the world? John the Baptist comes as an early witness, not as a consistent Helper. The male disciples are certainly not Helpers of Jesus; they are often presented as somewhat otiose travelling companions (see 4.27–38; 11.7–16). Even the beloved disciple is not a Helper; he seems to have a largely passive role. The women disciples are presented in a more positive light. The Samaritan woman conducts a very fruitful mission in her home town, Martha confesses Jesus as Christ, Mary anoints his feet, Mary Magdalene announces the news of Jesus' return to the Father. However, there is no sense in which any one of these women helps Jesus to fulfil his commission to bring life into the world. Even the Holy Spirit is not Jesus' Helper in any obvious sense. He rests on Jesus at the baptism and is said to remain (*meno*) with him. However, there are no allusions to Jesus performing various actions 'filled with the Holy Spirit', as there are for example in Luke's gospel.

The only other obvious candidate is God the Father. Is God Jesus' Helper? It is true that Jesus reveals his dependence upon the Father (see 5.30). The relationship between the Son and the Father is one of unanimity; the Son only does what he sees the Father doing. However, if John wants to depict the Father constantly helping Jesus in actually performing the deeds of God, he has failed in that endeavour. Jesus seems to exercise a lot of ingenuity to avoid giving the impression of divine assistance on a number of occasions. This is especially true in his prayers which are never cries for help, never petitionary in character. In 11.41–42, he prays to the Father before raising Lazarus. However, he is at pains to say that this is not because he needs the Father's help but because he wants the crowd to hear what he is praying. Then there is the prayer in 12.27:

> Now my heart is troubled, and what shall I say? 'Father, save me from this hour'? No, it was for this very reason I came to this hour. Father, glorify your name!

Here we get an inkling of the anxiety experienced by Jesus as he imagined his forthcoming death. He says 'Now my heart is troubled'. However, this does not lead him to throw himself on the mercy of God as in Luke 24.42. Far from it. Jesus rejects the prayer, 'Father, save me from this hour' and chooses instead to pray, 'Father, glorify your name!' Here, and in Chapter 17, there is no hint of Jesus asking the Father to help him through the impending ordeal (see also 18.11). *It is not easy, therefore, to argue that God is Jesus' Helper.*

We have to conclude that an obvious, consistent Helper is absent in the narrative of the fourth gospel. This raises an interesting question; 'Why has John portrayed Jesus as a man without obvious Helpers?' The answer has to do with John's understanding of Jesus' heroism. The quintessential hero in storytelling has always been the solitary and isolated individual who pits himself against apparently overwhelming forces. In this respect the hero has something of a superhuman even supernatural character; indeed, the word *heros* suggests this since it denotes someone who is literally half divine and half human. It is this superhuman and solitary heroism which John wants to evoke in his characterization of Jesus. This emerges with particular power in the passion narrative (John 18–19). In these chapters, Jesus' sovereign individualism is constantly under-lined. Thus, in contrast to what we find in the Synoptics, Jesus goes out to greet Judas and the arresting party (18.4), he confidently embraces the cup which the Father has given him (18.11), and he carries his own cross to Golgotha (19.16b). John portrays Jesus as a hero who has no need of Helpers. The Johannine Jesus has no need for angels in the garden nor Simon of Cyrene at Golgotha.

Returning to Greimas' model, we can now add the last axis (the axis of power) and see John's plot as a whole:

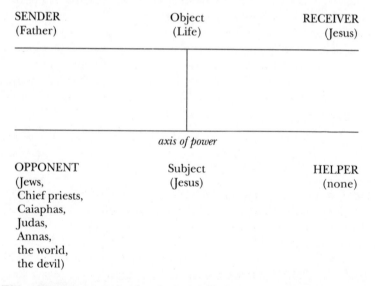

SENDER	Object	RECEIVER
(Father)	(Life)	(Jesus)

axis of power

OPPONENT	Subject	HELPER
(Jews,	(Jesus)	(none)
Chief priests,		
Caiaphas,		
Judas,		
Annas,		
the world,		
the devil)		

This diagram reveals the imbalance between Opponents and Helpers in Jesus' completion of his task. Jesus is depicted as the quintessential hero; the one who achieves his goal against all odds.

THE PARADOX IN JOHN'S PLOT

It may be felt that we have exhausted all there is to say about the main plot of the fourth gospel from an actantial perspective. However, we are not done yet. There is a surprise in store.

We may well agree that Greimas' actantial grid has proved helpful in revealing the deep structure of John's plot. John's story seems to obey what Greimas conceives to be the universal rules for storytelling. However, John's story also subverts this structure. As I have already indicated, there is a surprise in store. I have shown above that Jesus is a hero without any *obvious* Helpers. None of the characters who are seen to stand *with* Jesus are portrayed as ones who assist him in going to the cross to die for the world. But can this also be said of the characters who stand *against* Jesus? What about the Jewish hierarchy? Is there not a strange and paradoxical sense in which the Jews *help* Jesus to fulfil his mission? It is they who seek to arrest and kill him from Chapter 5 onwards. It is they who formally decide to have Jesus put to death in the council meeting at the end of Chapter 11. It is they who acquire the services of Judas and Pilate in the arrest and execution of Jesus. Is there not a sense in which Jesus depends upon the actions of his antagonists in order for his salvific death to occur?

My conviction is that John has a creative theodicy in which the evil forces at work in the gospel are seen to overreach their purposes and to contribute towards God's eternal plan. The devil is assuredly at work in John's narrative world, trying to persuade the Jews to kill Jesus, trying to persuade Judas to betray Jesus. Both the Jews and Judas actually fulfil the devil's intentions. However, the storyteller also makes it plain that it was God's will that Judas should betray Jesus, and that Jesus should be killed on a cross by the Jews! Jesus speaks of Judas in John 17.12 as 'the one *doomed* to destruction so that the Scripture would be fulfilled'. The narrator uses four Old Testament *testimonia* or proof texts to show how the crucifixion was part of God's purpose (19.24, 36–37). Indeed, the narrator takes care to reassure us with the formula, 'This happened so that the Scripture might be fulfilled'. In theological terminology, the antagonists of Jesus therefore contribute to the predetermined will of God. In narrative terminology, the antagonists of Jesus are both Opponent and Helper! Jesus' enemies help him to fulfil his commission. Indeed, without them, he *could not* have completed his work.

At this point I am conscious of a possible accusation of over-ingenuity, of the worst kind of literary-critical eisegesis. Surely, some may ask, this is much too subtle an effect for a storyteller like John! To readers who feel this way I can only say that the kind of ironic *peripeteia* (reversal of fortune) which I have just described is not uncharacteristic of ancient Hebrew storytelling. In 1971, the celebrated French structuralist Roland Barthes exposed the same dynamic in his actantial analysis of Genesis 32.22–32. In his essay, 'The Struggle with the Angel', Barthes looked at the story of Jacob wrestling with God using Greimas' actantial model of narrative (see Barthes 1977). His results were revealing. More than any biblical scholar before him, Barthes managed to show why it is, in narrative terms, that the reader experiences this story as 'a tale of the unexpected'.

Using Greimas' terminology, he showed how God is the Sender in the story, and Jacob is the Receiver. The commission is for Jacob to be reconciled with Esau. This in turn is Jacob's quest. Barthes argued that the Helper of this quest is God. The key thing for Barthes, however, is the fact that the Opponent is none other than God himself. The one who wrestles with Jacob is God; the Sender and the Opponent are one and the same. Barthes proposed that this kind of reversal is rare. Only blackmail stories ever have this kind of disorienting surprise. Barthes concluded that the story-teller of Genesis 32, in depicting the Sender and the Opponent as the same character, was in fact reinforcing the radical monotheism which we know was an essential element in Israelite theology. Barthes showed how Genesis 32 is in the truest sense narrative theology.

Returning to the deep structure of John's plot, we can now see the relevance of Barthes' thesis. In the plot of the fourth gospel we have discovered that the Opponent and the Helper are really one and the same. This highlights something significant about the nature of evil. Evil pushes people towards the most perverse and extreme conduct only to find that the eventual results contradict the evil intention. We see a graphic illustration of this in the death of Jesus. Here the devil compels the Jews and their assistants into killing the Giver of Life. What is ironic about their hostility is this: that in putting Jesus to death they are doing the very thing which will enable Jesus to cry out, 'It is finished!' The moment of their apparent triumph is therefore ironically the moment of their greatest failure! The Cross is, in reality, Jesus' triumphal exit.

A STRUCTURAL ANALYSIS OF JOHN'S COUNTER-PLOT

Greimas' model therefore provides us with a methodical means of examining the deep structures of John's main plot. The same can be said of our examination of John's counter-plot. It should be noted that there are really two plots going on in John's story and both take on the nature of quests. There is first of all the main plot, which is Jesus' quest to do the work of the Father. This has already been scrutinized in what I have written above. But there is also another plot. This is the quest of the Jews to destroy Jesus. This emerges in Chapter 5 (5.16) but is hinted at in 1.10–11, 2.13–22, and 4.1–3. This is a plot in the non-literary as well as the literary sense. In other words, it is a 'conspiracy'. The conspiracy to put the Giver of Life to death is the counter-plot in the fourth gospel. It is the negative quest which goes on at the same time as Jesus' positive quest to bring eternal life to a needy world.

Greimas' actantial model is valuable here because it helps to expose some of the satirical potential in this counter-plot. This satire consists of the fact that the quest of the Jews is presented as a parody of the quest of Jesus. Thus, if we look again at Greimas' model, we can see that the Sender in this counter-plot is the devil. By John 8 it becomes clear that the devil functions as 'the originator' behind the plot to kill Jesus. This is made explicit in John 8.31–59 when Jesus delivers a fierce invective against the Jews who had believed him. He says that they belong to their father who is the devil (8.44). The reason he can say that is because they are doing what their father does. Their father, the devil, has been a murderer from the beginning (8.44). Since the Jews are 'plotting' to kill Jesus, this reveals their true paternity. It shows that the devil, the murderer, is the 'Originator' of their actions. The fact that the chapter ends with the Jews trying to kill Jesus (8.59) just proves the point.

If the devil is the Originator, the Receivers are 'the Jews'. This group is given far more prominence than the chief priests, Pharisees, temple guards, Caiaphas, Annas and Judas so they alone are to be regarded as the actants fulfilling the role of Receivers. By speaking of 'the Jews' we are not referring to the Jewish nation as a whole nor to the crowds of Jews in Jerusalem. We are referring to the authorities responsible for the arrest and death of Jesus (Von Wahlde 1982: 44). As far as John is concerned, this group performs actions whose motivation originates in the twisted will of the devil. When Jesus says, 'you do what you have heard from your father' (8.38), his words give us an indication of the axis of commission in the counter-plot; the devil has told the Jews to kill Jesus.

In the axis of volition (the quest axis), the Jews are the Subject and their desire to put Jesus to death is the Object. As for the axis of power, the Opponent is evidently Jesus. The principal Helper acquired by the Jews in the fulfilling of this negative quest is Judas. Judas is interestingly one into whom Satan has entered (13.27). He is not only 'prompted by the devil' (13.2), he is now one with the devil. The Sender and the Helper are therefore one and the same.

Looking at the counter-plot as a whole, we can see these observations in diagrammatical form:

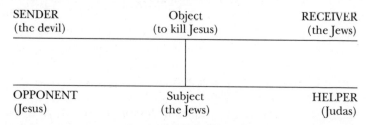

SENDER (the devil)	Object (to kill Jesus)	RECEIVER (the Jews)
OPPONENT (Jesus)	Subject (the Jews)	HELPER (Judas)

Perhaps the most revealing thing about this counter-plot is its satirical parody of the main plot. The devil's relationship to the Jews is a parody of the relationship between God and Jesus. This is brought out with particular poignancy by Jesus in 8.31–59. The relationship between the devil and the Jews is a Father–Son relationship, like that between God and Jesus. It is also a Sender–Receiver relationship (or more accurately, an Originator–Receiver relationship). To these Jews Jesus says, 'you do what you have heard from the Father'. The grim parody here consists of the fact that the Jews do what they hear their father saying, just as Jesus does.

Again we see the importance of actantial analysis for evoking some of these dynamics. Greimas' method has helped us to expose the way in which the relationship between the devil and the Jews functions as a sinister imitation of the relationship between the Father and the Son. In this matter I am reminded of a similar use of parody in Milton's *Paradise Lost*. In Book X we come across what can only be described as an 'unholy Trinity'. This consists of Satan, Sin and Death (Sin and Death are Satan's offspring). The Fall has now occurred and Sin and Death have been hard at work building a great bridge between Hell and Earth, over which Satan and his followers can travel more easily (ll.228ff). This activity is a parody of the description in Book VII of the work of the Holy Trinity (ll.210–242). Here the Son and the Spirit leave Heaven to create the world out of chaos. Tillyard points out some of the contrasts between Book VII and Book X:

> The divine Trinity is matched by the infernal Trinity of Satan, Sin and Death; and it is the second and third who do the work. The Holy Spirit broods like a dove over the abyss; Sin and Death hover over it like birds of prey. The Spirit creates through warmth and growth and purges away the intractable dregs. Death solidifies his causeway by chill and petrification, and the solid and slimy materials he uses are those very 'cold infernal dregs, adverse to life' which the Spirit had rejected. Generally the second passage is violent and excessive where the first passage is easy, though vast, and serene.
>
> (Tillyard 1969: 152–3)

The comparison between John and *Paradise Lost* is not a pointless one. It is intended to highlight John's satire of the Jews through a counter-plot which mimics the main plot. By making the Jews the Receiver and the devil the Sender, John has cleverly satirized the Jews, using the rhetoric of parody. This observation enables us to experience a modicum of aesthetic pleasure in those otherwise offensive passages where the Jews are condemned. As C.S. Lewis put it, 'it is a very old critical discovery that the imitation in art of unpleasing objects may be a pleasing imitation' (1979: 94). The use of parody in John's counter-plot enables the reader to enjoy this aspect of the gospel as a pleasing imitation of an unpleasing subject. In getting to this point of reader response, Greimas' categories have again proved useful.

A STRUCTURAL ANALYSIS OF JOHN'S MICRO-PLOTS

Thus far we have used Greimas' method for exposing the deep structure of John's macro plot sequences. That is to say, we have used the actantial grid to discern some of the literary subtleties of the two overall plots in John's story, the positive quest of Jesus on behalf of the Father, and the negative quest of the Jews on behalf of the devil. I now want to look at some micro-plots. These micro-plots are the plot sequences which we see in some of the individual narrative episodes, such as the story of the Baptist in John 1–3 and the attempt to arrest Jesus in John 7. We shall find that there are some interesting similarities between the pattern of these plots, and the pattern of the two plots of the gospel as a whole.

The story of John the Baptist (John 1.1–37; 3.23–36)

The story of John the Baptist, as portrayed in the opening chapters of the fourth gospel, is seen in a revealing light when exposed to an actantial approach. If we begin with the axis of communication, it is interesting to note that the Baptist, like Jesus, is a man sent from God. In the prologue, the narrator says, 'There came a man who was sent from God, his name was John' (1.6). Evidently the Sender is God the Father, the Receiver is the Baptist.

As far as the axis of volition is concerned, the Baptist is the Subject and the Object of his quest is to testify to Jesus. As the narrator explains, 'he came as a witness' (1.7). His role is to shout out '*Ide*', 'Look!' when the Messiah is near.

In doing this, the Baptist finds he has an Opponent. Here we come to the axis of power. He is challenged by the envoys sent by the Jews in Jerusalem. These envoys comprise priests, Levites and Pharisees. They subject John to an informal trial (1.19–28). In this respect, the opposition he faces acts as an anticipation of what Jesus will face. Jesus too will be subjected to many interrogations.

Interestingly enough, the Baptist has no obvious Helper in his mission. His disciples are not described as assisting him in any way. There is no obvious reference to God helping him at any point. Like Jesus, the Baptist stands alone. His is a solitary voice crying in the wilderness.

What we have in this paraphrase of the Baptist's story is an intimation, a rehearsal and an anticipation of the story of Jesus. The deep structure of the plot of the Baptist's story has resonances with the deep structure of the plot of the Messiah's story. Greimas' actantial approach has helped to confirm the point made by C.H. Dodd that 'each several episode . . . contains in itself, implicitly, the whole of the Gospel' (1965: 384).

So what happens to the Baptist has echoes with the story of Jesus. Both are 'sent from God' and in that sense Receivers. Both stand alone against an array of antagonists. In that sense they are faced by many Opponents (indeed, the same Opponents) and are unaided by obvious Helpers. Both are subjected to interrogations by the Jewish authorities in Jerusalem.

In terms of the deep plot-structure of the Baptist story, we can see that something of the plot of the Gospel as a whole is being imitated in the story of John the Baptist.

The Jews attempt to arrest Jesus (John 7)

If the story of the Baptist has structural similarities with the main plot of the gospel, the stories of the enemies of Jesus have structural similarities with the counter-plot in the gospel. As we have seen, the counter-plot consists of the devil (the Sender) urging the Jews (the Receiver/Subject) to arrest and kill Jesus (the Opponent/Object) with the assistance of Judas (the Helper). We see some echoes with this deep structure in the plot of John 7.

In John 7, the chief priests and the Pharisees are the Senders. They send the *huperetes* or temple guards to arrest Jesus (7.32). These *huperetes* are the Receivers and the object of their quest is to arrest Jesus, who is the Opponent.

The Helpers in John 7 are the Jews. They are first of all portrayed as looking for Jesus (7.11); secondly as listening out for pro-Jesus sentiments in the crowds (7.12–13); thirdly as questioning Jesus in the temple (7.15,35). The Jews are the front-stage Helpers of the Pharisees/chief priests who instigate the 'plot' behind the scenes (7.45). This, structurally speaking, resembles the counter-plot of John's gospel as a whole. In the latter, the devil is very much in the background, and yet at the same time manages to find Receivers who will attempt the task of putting Jesus to death in the fore-ground of the narrative.

Thus, just as the story of the Baptist resonates with the main plot, so the story of Jesus' enemies resonates with the counter-plot. Both micro-plot sequences have a hologrammatic function; they are parts which reflect the whole.

The function of John's use of plot

These insights concerning the structural aspects of John's plot are not supposed to imply that John is playing a subtle game with narrative techniques. In any event, it would be difficult to argue that John was entirely conscious of the interpretations offered here. What we can say is that John's construction of both macro- and micro-plot sequences is not to be regarded merely as an aesthetic adornment. Rather, it is geared to help the reader who comes to faith and decides to follow in the footsteps of Jesus. For the one whose reading of John's story proves transformative in this sense, the structural similarities between the stories of the Baptist and of Jesus imply that followers of Jesus can expect their own story of discipleship to follow a similar pattern. Their story will have a structural similarity with the story of Jesus. In this respect, John's work with plot sequences has a pastoral purpose.

Perhaps the most convincing evidence for this is Jesus' prediction of what will happen to his followers after the resurrection. What Jesus anticipates in the disciple's life is a story not unlike his own. After the ending of his own story, Jesus anticipates the beginning of a new and similar story in the life-history of his disciples.

This means, first of all, that the axis of commission in the story of the disciples will resemble the axis of commission in the story of Jesus. This is precisely what happens. Jesus portrays himself as a Sender to the disciples. As the Father has sent him, so he sends them (John 20.21). The relationship between Jesus and the disciples now imitates the relationship between the Father and the Son. It is a Sender–Receiver relationship.

This means, secondly, that the axis of volition in the story of the disciples will resemble the axis of volition in the story of Jesus. Thus Jesus calls the disciples to bear much fruit and fruit that lasts (John 15.1–17). They are to continue Jesus' mission of bringing life to those who accept their mission. In this respect, the disciples will continue the quest initiated by Jesus: life for the world.

Thirdly, the axis of power in the story of the disciples will resemble the axis of power in the story of Jesus. In Jesus' story, the opponents were Jews who wanted to put him to death. The disciples who continue Jesus' mission will find that the same kind of antagonism will await them. In 16.2 Jesus promises that the Jews 'will put you out of the synagogue; in fact a time is coming when anyone who kills you will think he is offering a service to God'. However, the disciples are to be comforted with the knowledge that this antagonism is a sign that their story is truly reflective of his own story. 'If they persecuted me, they will persecute you also' (15.20).

Even more importantly, the disciples are to be comforted with the knowledge that they will have a 'Helper' in this mission. They will have another *parakletos* (sometimes actually translated 'Helper') who will come to their aid and to their defence.

Using Greimas' actantial method, the story of the fourth gospel can therefore be seen as 'open-ended'. When the story of Jesus ends, the story of the disciples begins. This subsequent story will have many structural similarities with the story of Jesus, *except that the disciples will have a consistent and obvious Helper in the form of the parakletos.* In diagrammatical terms, the implied story of the disciples will look like this:

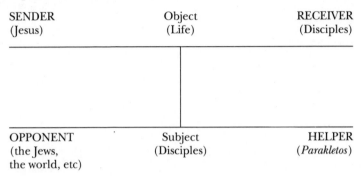

SENDER	Object	RECEIVER
(Jesus)	(Life)	(Disciples)

OPPONENT	Subject	HELPER
(the Jews, the world, etc)	(Disciples)	(*Parakletos*)

Conclusion

In this second chapter, we have looked at the plot of the fourth gospel. I began by refuting the common-sense theory of John's history-writing: that John merely reproduced his authoritative sources, and that his gospel therefore represents an entirely objective account of historical realities. Instead, I proposed that John's gospel is the product of a creative, historical imagination. In the case of the characterization of Jesus, John took hold of certain data suggestive of elusiveness and made that feature the over-arching key to understanding the Messiah. This process was an act of 'interpolation', of filling in the gaps in the sources and making a portrait of Jesus with inner consistency. In the case of his plot, John likewise selected and combined material into a narrative unity. This process was an act of 'comprehension', of imaginatively 'grasping together' various sayings and events in his sources (Mink 1970: 546). In that process, John linked material into a new causal, temporal and structural unity. Thus, in his creation of both 'hero' and 'plot', John has created something coherent and consistent.

Chapter 3

Genre

My argument thus far has highlighted John's creativity in the handling of his historical traditions. Whatever sources were available to him (and there is considerable debate on that subject), John has redescribed them so as to paint his own particular portrait of Jesus in a narrative with a clear sense of emplotment. In doing so, John must have been conscious of writing according to certain literary conventions. Some would argue that these conventions were simply those of Old Testament narrative; others that they were the universal conventions of storytelling (as delineated by Greimas). Many would want to say that John not only composed his gospel according to Jewish and even universal conventions, but also that he redescribed his story of Jesus in terms of a particular 'genre'. By 'genre' is meant 'a group of texts that exhibit a coherent and recurring configuration of literary features involving form (including structure and style), content and function' (Aune 1987: 13). All authors are mindful of the conventions of a particular genre when they set about the task of writing a story. We need to ask what genre dictated John's composition.

Discussion of the literary genre of the fourth gospel has been remarkably rare in twentieth century scholarship. Even in the last fifteen years, when literary approaches to John have emerged in strength, this topic has only occasionally been discussed. This is a surprising 'gap' in Johannine research. Establishing the genre of a work of literature is a vital part of the hermeneutical process. Indeed, identifying the genre of a work such as the fourth gospel is essential for a true understanding of its meaning. Failing to ask questions of genre is irresponsible. Assuming its genre is dangerous. Mistaking its genre can be disastrous. What is required is a careful study of the family resemblances between John's gospel and other known, ancient works in the great literary heritage prior to the gospel. The fourth gospel is not a totally new creation; no work of literature can claim the privilege of being *creatio ex nihilo*. John must therefore be examined in the light of those works with which it is most closely related.

THE GENRE OF THE SYNOPTIC GOSPELS

Needless to say, the most obvious family resemblance is between John and the gospels of Mark, Matthew and Luke (the Synoptics). Whatever one's view about the exact nature of the literary relationship between John and the Synoptics, it cannot be denied that John opted for a literary genre that was already in existence when he combined his traditions into a followable story. Whether he knew the Synoptics in their written form, or whether he had heard them in their oral form, the author of the fourth gospel was using a known genre, the 'gospel'.

The word 'gospel' (*evangelion* in Greek) is translated 'good news' in the NIV and refers to the message of salvation preached by the earliest Christians. Paul uses the noun approximately fifty times, and the verb twenty times, always to refer to the preaching of the 'good news' of Jesus Christ. By the time of the church fathers, however, the word 'gospel' was being used to refer to the actual four stories of Jesus by Mark, Matthew, Luke and John. No longer was it confined to the oral preaching of the good news. It now referred to a prose narrative which grew out of that preaching. This means that the word 'gospel' underwent an observable progression in denotation from 'the good news concerning, or as preached by, Jesus' to 'the written documents describing his preaching, ministry, passion and resurrection' (Burridge 1990: 266).

This may seem to have settled the matter very quickly. If John is a 'gospel', what more needs to be said about its genre? But it is precisely at this point that we come up against a major problem. For what is a gospel? It is one thing saying with conviction that John is a gospel. It is quite another answering with clarity what kind of literature is meant by the term 'gospel'. Is it something new, something *sui generis*, which grew out of the preaching of the good news? Or is it something which owes its existence to a particular genre of writing in antiquity?

The most thorough, recent attempt to provide some clarity in this area is Richard Burridge's book, *What are the Gospels?* (1992).

Burridge's hypothesis is that the four gospels are closest in kind to Graeco-Roman biographies, known as *Bioi* (*Vitae* in Latin). *Bios* itself is not a genre which can be rigidly separated from all other genres. Burridge points out that *Bios* is to be located on a spectrum, with history-writing at one extreme and encomium at the other. It also 'nestles' among genres such as rhetoric, moral philosophy, polemic and the novel (1992: 80). *Bios* is therefore a flexible genre.

David Aune, who has also written on the gospel genre, defines biography as 'a discrete prose narrative devoted exclusively to the portrayal of the whole life of a particular individual perceived as historical' (1987: 29). Burridge goes further than Aune by identifying the following generic features which occur within a flexible pattern: *Bios* will emerge from a group which has formed around a charismatic leader or teacher; its purpose will often be to combat some kind of teaching or social conflict; it will focus on one particular person, whose character is revealed through his words and deeds, and whose name is mentioned in the title or in the opening features; the tone will be respectful and serious; it will be written in prose narrative; it will usually be of medium length (about 7,000 words); it will also have a chronological structure.

Having identified the major characteristics of ancient *Bioi*, Burridge turns to the Synoptic gospels. He finds plenty of reasons for identifying these works as biographies. Mark, Matthew and Luke all emerged from a group of disciples who revered Jesus. They were all written in a community context. They were certainly written to meet needs in their author's churches; some of these needs were didactic. All three gospels focus on Jesus of Nazareth, whose name occurs in their opening features. A great deal of space is given to his teaching (in direct speech) and to the description of his actions. One period is given considerable attention: his passion and death. All three treat their subject with undisguised reverence. They write in prose narrative, with material selected from a range of oral and written units of tradition. All three are chronological in nature, having a clear sense of progression from the baptism of Jesus to his resurrection (in the case of Mark), and from his birth and childhood (in the case of Matthew and Luke). As Burridge concludes:

> There is a high degree of correlation between the generic features of Graeco-Roman *Bioi* and those of the synoptic gospels; in fact, they exhibit more of the features than are shown by works

at the edges of the genre, such as those of Isocrates, Xenophon and Philostratus.

(Burridge 1992: 218)

THE FOURTH GOSPEL AS BIOGRAPHY

When Burridge turns to the gospel of John, he argues that here too the family resemblance is with biography, and that John should be regarded as a *Bios Iesou*. This is not an altogether new insight. Fernando Segovia, a prolific literary critic of the fourth gospel, had already stated that he believed:

> that the Fourth Gospel does represent an example of ancient biography and, as such, follows the basic conventions of ancient biographical writings . . . I further believe that a proper atten-tion to and consideration of such biographical conventions can be very fruitful indeed in coming to terms with the plot of the Gospel.
>
> (Segovia 1991: 32)

Where Burridge supplements the work of Segovia is in his evidence for designating John as an example of biography. As in the case of his chapter on the Synoptics, Burridge is extremely thorough.

He argues that the fourth gospel grew out of a community context, and that this Johannine community was conversant with Hellenistic as well as Jewish culture. He further argues that the community responsible for this gospel had access to a number of written and oral traditions concerning Jesus. The social setting, occasion and purpose of John are all consistent with Graeco-Roman biography (1992: 221, 234–237).

From these sociological features, Burridge turns to the gospel itself. He argues that the following features are consonant with *Bioi*:

1 The title, *Kata Iohannen* ('According to John'). Since this is exactly the same construction as is used for the titles of each of the Synoptics, Burridge argues that it was perceived from the earliest days as 'of the same literary type' as them (1992: 222).
2 Opening features. Burridge notes that the name 'Jesus Christ' occurs in the prologue but not until v.17. After the prologue, the name Jesus appears ubiquitously. This again is consonant with *Bioi* such as the *Agricola*.
3 Verb subjects. Over half of the verbs in John are taken up with

Jesus' words and actions (55.3 per cent). This compares favourably with the Synoptics (Mark: 44.6 per cent; Matthew: 59.7 per cent; Luke: 54.7 per cent). John places less teaching on Jesus' lips than Matthew and Mark do (in spite of impressions to the contrary), but gives Jesus more prominence in his narrative overall. So John displays 'the same exaggerated skew effect which is typical of *Bioi* in both Jesus' activity in the narrative, as well as in the large amount of his teaching' (Burridge 1992: 224).

4 Allocation of space. Twenty per cent of John is devoted to the last supper, the passion and resurrection of Jesus. This again compares favourably with *Bioi*. 17.3 per cent of *Cato Minor* is devoted to the last days of the protagonist, and 26.3 per cent of *Apollonius of Tyana* to the imprisonment, trial and death of Apollonius.

5 Narrative settings. Burridge points out that the geographical settings in the fourth gospel are determined largely by the whereabouts of Jesus. This is a typical feature of *Bioi*.

6 Topics. John has the same kind of topics as ancient biographies (interest in Jesus' ancestry, and in his great deeds), though it has no interest in one common biographical topic: the birth, boyhood and education of Jesus.

7 Style. The style of John's gospel is Koine Greek, not high-flown or literary Greek (op. cit. p.233). 'Such a style is comparable to that in which popular *Bioi* or treatises were written' (op. cit. p.233).

8 Atmosphere. This is serious and respectful, as in *Bioi*.

9 Quality of characterization. John's portrayal of Jesus is a mixture of stereotype and realism. This is again typical of Graeco-Roman *Bioi*.

From these internal features, we move to external features. The first of these is the mode of representation. As is common in *Bioi*, John's mode is continuous prose narrative with extended discourses and dialogues. The second is size. John's gospel is 15,416 words in length, which is similar to *Cato Minor*. The third is structure. John has a chronological framework with topical material inserted, which again is typical of the structure found in many *Bioi* (op. cit. p.226). Fourth is scale. The focus in John is very much on Jesus; he rarely leaves the stage. This again is typical. Fifth is the literary units. Burridge argues that 'the Fourth Gospel is composed mainly of stories, dialogues and speeches or discourses, which are material typical of *Bioi*, especially those of philosophers and teachers' (op.

cit. p.227). Sixth is sources. Here again John's use of oral and written sources is the approach of the writers of *Bioi*, especially those who wrote about philosophers and teachers. Finally is 'methods of characterization'. In John, as in *Bioi*, the author's main strategy is to reveal character through deeds and words.

Having marshalled all this evidence, Burridge writes, 'The hypothesis that the Fourth Gospel is a *Bios Iesou* is thus confirmed' (op. cit. p.238).

CRITIQUE OF THE *BIOS* HYPOTHESIS

Burridge's argument is cumulative and compelling. Looked at in terms of the statistics which he so carefully assembles, the hypothesis that John intended to write a kind of *Bios Iesou* is indeed plausible. It is, not, however, without problems. Some would prefer to see John's gospel in terms of Old Testament genres. As David Aune writes, 'those who favour an Old Testament model for the literary pattern(s) of the Gospels usually focus on either the Moses stories of the Pentateuch or the Elijah–Elisha cycle' (Aune 1987: 38). This is what we find in contemporary research on John's gospel. In a recent literary and historical study of the fourth gospel, Meg Davies has included a chapter on 'genre', but she contends that the genre of the fourth gospel is modelled on Old Testament narratives. She proposes that John depicts Jesus as a prophet like Moses and that 'the motifs, vocabulary, arrangement and genre of the Fourth Gospel are explained by reference to Scripture' (Davies 1992: 88).

Davies focuses on John's use of Scripture. She stresses John's use of Moses traditions deriving from Exodus and Deuteronomy; John's life of Jesus is patterned, in part, on the life of Moses. She also draws attention to the similarities between John's narrative and the stories of Elijah and Elisha. The healings of Jesus seem in particular to have been modelled on those performed by Elijah and Elisha. A short section is also devoted to the Wisdom literature, and comparisons between the activities and mission of Jesus with that of *Sophia* (Wisdom) in the Old Testament and intertestamental literature are suggested.

Davies then turns to what she calls 'non-Jewish Hellenistic portraits of religious leaders' (1992: 90). She is willing to allow that some of the material in John can be said to mirror Dionysian stories (1992: 88, 90, 100). However, comparisons with Graeco-Roman biographies do not bear fruit, in her opinion. Indeed, Davies is very guarded about calling John's gospel a *Bios Iesou*. She writes:

> Unfortunately, the biography which is most like the New Testament Gospels, Philostratus' *Life of Apollonius of Tyana*, is late, published in 217 CE, and may itself have been influenced by the Gospels.
>
> (Davies 1992: 103)

She goes on to stress:

> When we compare the account of Apollonius' life with that of Jesus in the Fourth Gospel . . . the differences are more apparent than the similarities.
>
> (Davies 1992: 103)

Davies concludes that there are only tenuous links with Hellenistic biographies of religious leaders, but that these links would have 'opened the Gospel to Greek readers ignorant of Johannine Scriptures' (p.104).

In the light of Davies' views, we can see that there are currently two extremes in genre criticism of the fourth gospel. At one end of the critical spectrum is Richard Burridge, who claims that John's gospel is a Graeco-Roman biography with strong Jewish elements. At the other end is Meg Davies, who proposes with equal vigour that the fourth gospel is an example of Jewish narrative theodicy, with enough elements of Graeco-Roman biography to make it accessible to Greek readers. How are we to move beyond this problem?

JOHN: A HELLENISTIC-JEWISH WORK

The first thing to do is to move away from an either/or mentality; in other words, that the fourth gospel is either Hellenistic or Jewish. Clear and strong demarcations between Hellenism and Judaism are inadvisable in the study of religion known as 'the history of religions approach' (*Religionsgeschichte*), especially when we look at first century Palestine. As Gerald Downing writes:

> A great many Jews in the period designated [the intertestamental and New Testament era] lived away from Judea and Galilee, were involved in the Greek world, spoke Greek, and often lacked any knowledge of Hebrew or Aramaic. At least some of the questions that concerned them were questions raised amongst Greeks.
>
> (Downing 1990: 277)

Scholars interested in *Religionsgeschichte* have therefore become very cautious of imposing a Greek-Hebrew divide on the varied cultures of the first century.

We would do well to bear this in mind in any genre-critical approach to the fourth gospel. John's gospel, like all the New Testament documents, was written in Greek for people whose normal language was Greek. John's quotations from the Old Testament are from the Greek translation known as the Septuagint, not from the Maseoretic text which was written in Hebrew. On many occasions, John assumes that his readers will need to have Aramaic terms translated, Jewish customs explained, and Palestinian geography described. Here are a number of examples from the first four chapters alone:

1.38: They said 'Rabbi' (which means Teacher).

1.41: 'We have found the Messiah' (that is, the Christ).

1.42: 'You will be called Cephas' (which, when translated, is Peter).

2.6: Nearby stood six stone water jars, the kind used by the Jews for ceremonial washing . . .

3.23: Now John was also baptising at Aenon near Salim, because there was plenty of water.

4.9: (For Jews do not associate with Samaritans).

4.25: 'I know that Messiah' (called Christ) 'is coming . . .'

Such narratorial asides are only really explicable if John was writing for a predominantly Greek-speaking readership which either needed educating or reminding about Palestinian vocabulary, customs and geography.

However, it is also true that John's gospel seems to have been written by a Jewish Christian for Jewish Christians! Recent scholarship has highlighted the Jewishness of John's gospel. For example, the stark dualisms of light and darkness, of truth and error, were felt to be Hellenistic in origin until the discovery of the Dead Sea scrolls. It is now clear that the Qumran community used precisely this kind of dualism, and that the language of Jesus in the fourth gospel is much closer to the kind we find in the Jewish sect at Qumran. This shows the extent to which John thinks as a Jew. Indeed, his indebtedness to the Old Testament Scriptures, his presentation of Jesus in terms of Wisdom, his use of rabbinic homiletic devices (see John 6) all point to the new consensus that most of the parallels with John's thought are to be found in Palestinian Judaism as well as in Hellenistic culture.

If the Jewishness of the author has been established, so the Jewishness of his readership has recently been asserted. Many scholars agree that John was published in the last decade of the first century, and was first and foremost a pastoral document written to encourage Jewish Christians who had been excommunicated from the synagogues because of their faith in Jesus. Until about 85 CE, Jewish Christians continued to worship with their non-Christian, Jewish families in the diaspora synagogues. However, in about 85 CE, an edict was issued from Jamnia encouraging all local synagogues to root out and expell the 'Nazarene heretics', those who believed in Jesus. From this moment on, Jewish Christians either renounced their Christianity or they relinquished their Judaism. Those who decided they wanted to remain within the fold of Judaism simply became apostates (or tried to stay within Judaism as crypto-Christians). Those who decided they wanted to follow Jesus lost everything that we commonly hold dear: home, family and security. It is mainly to the latter that John's gospel is addressed.

The evidence therefore suggests that the original readership of the fourth gospel was mainly made up of Greek-speaking Jewish Christians who needed to be encouraged 'to go on believing that Jesus is the Christ, the Son of God' (John 20.31). This readership was formed into a separate community as a result of the excommunication of many of its members from the synagogues. It had also opened its doors to Samaritans and Greeks (John 4.4–42; 12.20–22). For this reason, the fourth gospel is both Jewish and Hellenistic in many of its features. On the one hand John feels the need to explain the most basic Jewish customs and vocabulary. On the other hand, the same author uses some of the most fundamental, Jewish thought-forms. This also applies to the genre of the gospel. On the one hand John arranged his material into what, in the most general terms, would be recognized by Greeks as a kind of *Bios Iesou*. On the other hand, he used Old Testament traditions in the most sophisticated way so as to make his protagonist meaningful to Jews.

THE GENERIC DEPTHS OF JOHN'S GOSPEL

One of the problems with Burridge and Davies is that their theories do not account for the 'classic' appeal of John's gospel. Those who stress that John's gospel is *just* an example of Hellenistic biography, or *just* an example of Jewish theodicy, leave the reader asking, 'Then how come this gospel has always been regarded as a religious classic – sometimes *the* religious classic – by such a wide range of readers?' To say that John's gospel is simply biography or theodicy will appear all too reductionist for readers who regard John in this light. For them, John's gospel is a fecund combination of both Hellenistic and Jewish literary features. As David Aune writes, 'the canonical Gospels constitute a distinctive type of ancient biography combining (to oversimplify slightly) Hellenistic form and function with Jewish content' (1987: 22). But even this more comprehensive perspective is not entirely satisfactory, for Aune's definition does not explain the universal and perennial appeal of John's story for those who know nothing of Greek biography and Jewish theodicies. Where does this classic appeal come from?

From a literary-critical perspective, the abiding appeal of the fourth gospel has something to do with its creative use of generic modes. Put another way, the plot of the gospel has been structured in such a way as to resonate with the archetypes of storytelling. These archetypal patterns have been described by Northrop Frye as the four essential *mythoi* or modes to be found in world literature (1971: 163–242). They are romance, tragedy, anti-romance and comedy. They appear in literature with the frequency and the cyclicity of the seasons. That is why Frye associates romance with summer, tragedy with autumn, anti-romance (by which he means 'satire' and 'irony') with winter, and comedy with spring. Seen as a whole, Frye's system of archetypal modes looks like this:

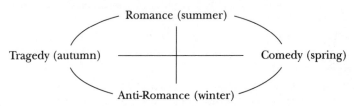

Frye argues that all literary texts, as soon as they tell a story, can be located somewhere in this system of narrative. Their plots will resonate with at least one of these four modes. Indeed, no writer can create a completely new story-form because s/he is subject to the coordinating power of these generic modes: romance, tragedy, satire/irony and comedy. As such, a primary task of literary interpretation must be the identification of the *mythos* employed by a storyteller. From here, true appreciation can begin.

What is revealing about the fourth gospel is this: that when it is read as *literature*, all four of these modes emerge in the plot of the story. If we begin with the story of summer (romance), it is noteworthy that Alan Culpepper, in his seminal study of the literary design of the fourth gospel, proposes that the plot of John's gospel, observed as a whole, resembles a romance. He starts with Frye's definition of a romance as a successful quest with three main stages: 'the preliminary minor adventures; the crucial struggle, usually some kind of battle in which either the hero or his foe, or both, must die; and the exaltation of the hero' (Frye 1971: 187). These three stages can be summed up as *agon* (conflict), *pathos* (death scene) and *anagnorisis* (recognition). Culpepper proposes that we can discern the three stages of the romance *mythos* in the plot of John's gospel:

> In the Gospel of John, Jesus, who has descended from the world above, is unrecognized except by a privileged few. As he strives to fulfil his mission, preliminary minor 'adventures' (i.e. signs and conflicts with opponents) begin to reveal his identity. He is faced with a crucial struggle, his own death, which he accepts and thereby finishes his task successfully: 'It is finished' (19.30).
>
> Although triumph takes the form of apparent defeat, he is recognized by his followers as 'my Lord and God' (20.28).
>
> (Culpepper 1983: 83)

Though Culpepper admits that 'the fit is not perfect' (1983: 84), his analysis certainly reveals elements of 'summer' in the story of the fourth gospel.

Whilst Culpepper argues for the *mythos* of romance, a much larger group of scholars have, throughout this century, argued that the plot of the fourth gospel resembles tragedy (Hitchcock 1911, 1923; Bowen 1930; Connick 1948; Lee 1953; Pierce 1960; Flanagan 1981; Domeris 1983; Malina 1985). At the heart of 'the archetypal myth of tragedy' (Frye 1979: 211) is the tragic hero, who 'is somewhere between the divine and the "all too human"' (Frye 1971: 207). This figure behaves in such a way that an act of revenge is provoked. The act of revenge is the *pathos*, a spectacle of extreme suffering, which takes on the form of a sacrifice. Indeed, Frye contends that 'Anyone accustomed to think archetypally of literature will recognize in tragedy a mimesis of sacrifice' (1971: 214).

No wonder, then, that scholars have associated the plot of the fourth gospel with what Frye calls the tragic *mythos*. Everything in John's gospel builds up to the sacrifice of the divine-human hero on the cross, and in that respect there is something *archetypally* tragic about its story. As Maud Bodkin once wrote: 'St John's image of the God-Man possesses for us its appealing and tragic glory' (1978: 288). Why? Because: 'In Christ appears pre-eminently this character felt obscurely in such heroes of poetic tragedy as Oedipus and Lear' (1978: 284).

If the plot of the fourth gospel seems to draw from the genres of romance and tragedy, it also draws from the genre of satire and irony. Little time needs to be spent on satire because, in Chapter 5, I will highlight the presence of 'informal satire' in John's Gospel. Certainly in John 8.31–59, Jesus as portrayed as a satirical iconoclast who exposes, in the most savage language, the spiritual blindness of a group of Jews who defect from him.

Some comments are required, however, on irony. Many scholars have highlighted the prevalence of irony in the plot of the fourth gospel (Clavier 1959; Wead 1970, 1974; MacRae 1973; Culpepper 1983; Duke 1985; Kotze 1985; O'Day 1986; Myers 1988; Botha 1991a, 1991b). Irony, at its simplest, thrives on the contrast between what the characters in the narrative world fail to understand (because of their limited perspective) and what the reader outside the narrative world understands (because of an omniscient perspective granted by the narrator). In John's gospel, this contrast is exploited on every page. In every episode of the gospel, we (the readers) see things about Jesus which the characters in the story miss. Most foundational of all these ironies is the fact that the Jews reject the Messiah they are so eagerly awaiting! John's irony orginates in what Aristotle called *agnoia* – a failure of recognition. The Jews in Jerusalem fail to recognize that Jesus of Nazareth is their Messiah.

What, finally, of the *mythos* of spring, comedy? Meg Davies, in her genre-critical chapter on John quoted earlier, states with confidence that 'It is immediately obvious that the Fourth Gospel is not a comedy' (1992: 67). To be sure, there is little which a reader will find funny in the story of the fourth gospel. But there is more to comedy than laughter. Leland Ryken, who also uses Frye's system of literature but on the Bible as a whole, defines the shape of the comic plot as follows:

The overall progression is from problem to solution, from bondage to freedom. The plot consists of a series of obstacles that must be overcome en route to the happy ending.

(Ryken 1974: 82)

Comedy is, then, a story with a U-shaped plot. The action involves a descent into a series of obstacles, before ascending to a happy resolution, usually signalled by a wedding, a feast, or a reconciliation scene. Such an outline is again descriptive of the plot of John's gospel. Jesus descends from heaven, is met by a number of obstacles, is killed but then raised from the dead, before ascending to heaven. This, in essence, is the U-shaped plot of comedy.

There are therefore grounds for arguing that the plot of the fourth gospel is similar in shape to romance, tragedy, satire/irony and comedy, as Northrop Frye describes them. However, we must be cautious about jumping to conclusions too quickly. There is a danger in abstractions; sooner or later, if one generalizes about a genre with sufficient vagueness, almost any work of literature can be described as an example. A more nuanced approach would be to argue that none of Frye's four genres is the single *mythos* on which John is drawing. John's gospel is not a romance; 'There is a sense of dreamy wistfulness in romances like *The Faerie Queene* which we certainly do not sense in John's gospel' (Stibbe 1992: 126). John's gospel is not a tragedy; whilst the passion and death of Jesus have elements of tragedy, the overall plot is U-shaped and therefore nearer to comedy. However, comedy itself will not do as a totally satisfying generic description; there is too much unresolved conflict and a total absence of reconciliation between hero and opponents to justify that claim. Likewise, John's gospel cannot be summed up as either satire or irony; while there are episodes in which Jesus and the narrator use satire and irony to vilify Jesus' antagonists, neither of these words will do as an overall description of the gospel's genre.

A more subtle explanation would be as follows: that the plot of the fourth gospel makes creative use of all four of these generic modes at different points. The story proper begins on a note of comedy (John 2.1–11). The wedding at Cana of Galilee has misunderstanding, the implication of drunkenness and feasting, the Dionysian motif of wine, and the ignorance of the chief steward. All these are comic ingredients. Indeed, the whole episode takes place just prior to the springtime festival of Passover (John 2.13).

As Hitchock wrote of John 1.19–2.11, 'the very air of these early scenes is spring, the budding life of the year, in the buoyant sunshine when men's hearts are most ready and eager for a change of life' (1923: 17). The fourth gospel therefore starts with a story suggestive of the *mythos* of spring.

This beginning, however, presents us with a paradox. Weddings usually occur at the conclusion of comic stories, as the final expression of the story's *eucatastrophe* ('happy ending'). As Frye points out, weddings are the most common party or festive ritual at the end of comic dramas (1971: 163). The paradox of John's story is the fact that, in archetypal terms, the gospel *begins with an episode associated with happy endings.* Now there is a reason for this, so the reader should be surprised but not disoriented. John portrays Jesus as the one who introduces the things reserved for the 'last day' into the now of history; he raises the dead and pronounces judgement, actions expected from God at the very end of time. By starting his gospel with a happy ending, John expresses through narrative form what he is trying to make as a theological claim; that the end has arrived now, in the person of Jesus!

In the episodes following the wine miracle, the *mythos* is more suggestive of romance. After the marriage motif is introduced at John 2.1–11, the reader senses romance in the air. This atmosphere is further strengthened by John the Baptist's description of Jesus as 'the bridegroom' and himself as 'the bridegroom's friend':

> The bride belongs to the bridegroom. The friend who attends the bridegroom waits and listens for him, and is full of joy when he hears the bridegroom's voice. That joy is mine, and it is now complete.
>
> (John 3.29)

Here the Baptist is using Old Testament metaphors associated with the future Messianic era, when Yahweh would be wed with his people in an eschatological marriage. Jesus is the bridegroom; the Baptist is the best man. But who, then, is the bride in 3.29?

At this point John tells a story of an encounter between Jesus and a Samaritan woman. It is high noon (John 4.6) and the scene is therefore set for a story influenced by the *mythos* of summer. The heat of the summer sun is oppressive, and Jesus is thirsty. He speaks to the woman who is drawing water from a well. The subject eventually turns to marriage. She has been married five times and is now living with a sixth man. This makes Jesus the seventh and therefore perfect man in her life. A symbolic betrothal is now suggested. The woman of Samaria becomes the eschatological bride. At the same well where Jacob was betrothed to Rachel, the woman of Samaria becomes the 'bride' in the long-awaited marriage between God and his people. The surprise, of course, is that she is not Jewish; she is a Samaritan, and 'Jews do not associate with Samaritans' (4.9). This indicates that the new era inaugurated by the Messiah will be universal rather than narrowly nationalistic. All who follow Jesus can be a part of this new age, whether they are Jews, Greeks, Samaritans or any other race. No longer is Israel alone the bride of Yahweh.

In John 2–4, therefore, the author uses and subverts the *mythoi* of comedy and romance. In John 5–10, the *mythos* changes from summer to winter. This section of the gospel contains violent arguments between Jesus and the Jews, and builds up to the climactic debate in John 10.22–39, where Jesus declares, 'I and the Father are one' (10.30). It is in this section of the gospel that satire comes to the fore. Here Jesus satirizes the Jewish leaders and the Jewish apostates for their lack of faith and insight. It is also here that the gospel's irony is most visible, as the Messiah walks unrecognized amidst his people, and as Jesus the judge is constantly placed 'on trial' by the Jewish authorities. No wonder we find the narrator saying, in the final episode of this section, that 'It was winter' (John 10.22). Truly, the biting *mythos* of satire and irony is most visible in this section. From the springtime merriment of Cana, and the summertime romance of Samaria, we have come to the wintery hostility of Jerusalem.

After the *peripeteia* in John 11–12 (the change of fortune caused by the raising of Lazarus and the triumphal entry), John turns to the *mythos* of autumn. Now, in John 13–17, he develops the mood into one of tragedy. The *agon* or conflict of John 5–10 has sealed Jesus' fate. The events at Bethany in 11.1–44 have caused Caiaphas to pronounce that Jesus must die. Now, like Socrates in Plato's *Phaedo*, Jesus bids farewell to his immediate followers. The atmosphere is solemn, the tone of Jesus' words is valedictory. The disciples are, by and large, quiet. After the warnings have ended in John 16, and after Jesus has prayed in John 17, Jesus and his disciples go to the garden where he is arrested. He is bound and taken to Annas where he is interrogated and struck. He is taken on to Caiaphas and then to Pilate, where he is dressed up in the humiliating garb of a mock-king and flogged. He is handed over to be crucified after a farce of a trial. He is executed between two thieves in the macabre scenery of a setting called Golgotha, 'the place of the skull'. Soldiers cast lots for the pitiful quantity of his possessions, a seamless tunic and some other garments. Jesus utters his final instructions to family and friends before he cries, 'It is finished', and dies.

The death of Jesus is John's gospel is presented as a kind of *pathos*, the scene of suffering in which the hero is sacrificed in tragedy. Though John describes the sufferings of Jesus in the sparsest manner, the passion is still a tragic story. Tragedy originates in stories of dying gods like Dionysus. As Frye writes:

> Tragic stories, when they apply to divine beings, may be called Dionysiac. These are stories of dying gods, like Hercules with his poisoned shirt and his pyre, Orpheus torn to pieces by the Bacchantes, Balder murdered by the treachery of Loki, Christ dying on the cross. . . .
>
> (Frye 1971: 36)

The death of Jesus in John's gospel is archetypally tragic. The kingship of Jesus is stressed throughout the account. The deity of Jesus has been firmly established already in the gospel. In John 18–19, we see *in history* what human beings had already expressed in pre-Christian myths and tragedies: the killing of the king, the story of the dying god. Here, in John's passion narrative, the awful nightmare comes true. Human beings, who should have recognized the true identity and mission of Jesus, commit deicide.

But this is not the end of the story. The death of Jesus is portrayed as a 'lifting up' in John's gospel. It is presented as one aspect of the hour of Jesus' return. It is therefore part of the upward curve of John's U-shaped plot. It is not a desperate conclusion to the story. It is the necessary means of Jesus' departure and ascent to glory. So in John 20, we return to where we began – with the *mythos* of comedy. We are again in the springtime, a week after Passover. Various disciples are looking for Jesus' body at the tomb. Mary Magdalene, in particular, seeks Jesus like the woman seeking her lover in the Song of Songs (3.1–4). Weeping, she searches for her loved one in a garden outside the city. She sees someone whom she mistakes for a gardener. But it is Jesus, risen and alive! In the springtime season of rebirth, Jesus has been raised from death. Like a grain of wheat which dies, but then produces many seeds (John 12.24), Jesus has returned as the firstfruits of the resurrection of the dead. So the ending of the gospel is a happy one after all. Like the best comic stories, the one who was lost is found, the one who had died returns to life. Mary can shout with joy, 'I have seen the Lord!'

CONCLUSION

David Tracy defined a classic as a text which so discloses a compelling truth about our lives that we cannot deny it some kind of normative status. These texts produce a disclosure of reality which 'surprises, provokes, challenges, shocks and eventually transforms us' (1981: 108). Religious classics like the fourth gospel also produce these kinds of reactions. Such texts have a disclosive power. They shock us into recognizing our finitude, our mortality, our sinfulness, our rage for order. They awaken wonder, trust, loyalty, justice, love or faith (1981: 164). However, such responses are only elicited in readers who approach such classics as literature. To use Martin Buber's terminology, there must be an I–Thou relationship with the gospel, not an I–It divorce. In this endeavour, literary criticism of the gospels is, for Tracy, a giant step in the right direction. As he puts it:

> When we approach these confessing narratives *as narratives* . . . with the aid of literary-critical methods, we can begin to see their fuller religious and existential significance.
>
> (Tracy 1981: 278)

In this chapter I have often described John's story of Jesus as a 'classic'. Here is a narrative which, if read with trust rather than resistance, can awaken the Christological confession, 'My Lord and my God!' (John 20.28). But what is it that gives John's story of Jesus the status of 'religious classic'? The argument of this chapter is that it is, at least in part, the genre of the gospel which contributes towards this recognition. Those who insist that John's gospel is merely a *Bios Iesou* have only grasped one aspect of the gospel's generic matrix. Those who insist that it is a story modelled after Old Testament narratives – the Moses story, or the Elijah–Elisha cycle – have only grasped another. The fact is, the gospel of John is, in generic terms, all of these and probably much more. It is a story which seems to reverberate with some of the deepest, archetypal patterns in romance, tragedy, satire and comedy.

It is for this reason that I am unhappy with the discussion of genre in literary studies of John to date. Such discussions pay too little attention to the generic influences upon the plot of the fourth gospel. Yet this is unwise. Hayden White has shown that historians explain history by giving to events a sense of 'emplotment' (his term). By emplotment, White means the encoding of facts into specific plot-structures. White argues that 'no given set of casually recorded historical events themselves constitute a story; the most they can offer to the historian are story elements' (1978: 47). It is up to the historian to match up a specific plot-structure with the set of historical events which he wishes to endow with meaning.

White proposes that the plot-structures available to an historian are those described by Northrop Frye:

> Following the line indicated by Northrop Frye in his *Anatomy of Criticism*, I identify at least four different modes of emplotment: Romance, Tragedy, Comedy and Satire.
>
> (White 1973: 7)

White goes on to add that:

> These four archetypal story forms provide us with a means of characterizing the different kinds of explanatory effects a historian can strive for on the level of narrative emplotment.
>
> (White 1973: 10)

He argues that events are not intrinsically romantic, tragic, comic or satirical. But viewed from a certain perspective, they can be perceived as (let us say) tragic and articulated in a way that resonates with the archetypal, tragic *mythos*.

White's metahistorical system is extremely helpful in relation to the genre of John's gospel. What White is arguing is that an historian emplots historical sequences in terms that are romantic, tragic, comic or satirical (or a subtle blending of two or more of these). As an example, he draws attention to the differences between the ways in which Michelet and Tocqueville tell the story of the French revolution. Michelet uses a plot-structure reminiscent of romance whilst Tocqueville uses one which is reminiscent of ironic tragedy (1978: 48).

My conviction is that John does the same kind of thing with his narrative historiography of Jesus. He draws on all four archetypes – first comedy, then romance, then satire and irony, then tragedy, before finally returning to comedy. Knowing Frye's system of archetypes, and White's application of it to history, helps us to characterize the effects which John-the-historian achieves at the level of emplotment. It also helps us to understand the generic subtleties of the fourth gospel.

In the final analysis I agree with Aune that the fourth gospel is in form an example of Hellenistic biography and in content very like stories of Moses and other Jewish, charismatic heroes. However, John also employs the archetypal modes of storytelling in general: comedy, romance, satire/irony and tragedy. Only such a comprehensive account of the genre of the fourth gospel begins to explain, on literary grounds, why this story continues to hold all kinds of readers under its spell.

Chapter 4

Style

One aspect of the fourth gospel which has been illuminated by recent literary methods is that of 'style'. If you look at the major commentaries up until 1990, they usually include a small section on the style of John's gospel in their introductions. What is striking about these discussions is their complete lack of attention to the *narrative* dynamics of the gospel. Traditional commentaries do not consider issues like plot, characterization, narrator, point of view, focalization, narrative genre, and so on. Commentaries like that of C.K. Barrett (1978) show more interest in John's Greek, vocabulary, key words (e.g. *agape*, sacrificial love), use of parataxis and asyndeton, characteristic verbal constructions, interplay of narrative and discourse, use of poetry, and structure. None of these matters is irrelevant to John's 'style' and any discussion of this topic must include some reference to the kind of features identified by Barrett and others. But if this is all that is said of John's literary characteristics the discussion is likely to be severely impoverished. There is much more to John's narrative art than the use of key words and favourite Greek constructions.

The one method which can contribute more than any other to our appreciation of John's style is that of narrative criticism. Narrative criticism really emerged with the publication of Alan Culpepper's seminal book, *Anatomy of the Fourth Gospel: A Study in Literary Design* (1983). In this major work, Culpepper introduced a fresh approach to the literary characteristics of John's gospel. Drawing on some of the principal narrative theorists of our time (particularly Gerard Genette), Culpepper studied the narrator and point of view in John (Chapter 2), John's use of narrative time (Chapter 3), the evidences of plot in the gospel (Chapter 4), John's method of characterization (Chapter 5), the presence of 'implicit commentary' (Chapter 6), and the device of the implied reader (Chapter 7). Culpepper, more than any other scholar, helped readers to see the style of John's narrative from an entirely modern (perhaps even post-modern) perspective. From 1983 onwards, no self-respecting scholar of the fourth gospel could afford to ignore his book.

Since the publication of *Anatomy*, I have tried to take the discussion of John's style further by refining Culpepper's narrative-critical method. In my book *John as Storyteller*, subtitled 'Narrative Criticism and the Fourth Gospel' (1992), I applauded Culpepper whilst criticizing him for his neglect of the historical features of the fourth gospel. I pointed out how critical Culpepper had been of historical criticism in his opening, introductory chapter. In a much quoted remark, he compared historical critics to archaeologists who regard the gospel as a tell to be dug up and separated into different strata or layers. Culpepper's approach was to be different. Rather than focus on what putatively lies behind the text, he preferred to concentrate on the final form and to treat that as an autonomous narrative world. No consideration of the historical dimensions of the gospel was to be included. The gospel was to be treated as a mirror, not as a window on to the history of Jesus or on to the Johannine church.

In *John as Storyteller* I questioned aspects of this methodology and argued that Culpepper was drawing in an uncritical way on the assumptions of New Criticism. I took him respectfully to task for not recognizing the sociological and historical functions of narrative. There has, after all, been a great deal written in recent years on the ways in which communities employ narrative as a device for enhancing social values and corporate identity. There has also been a great deal written about the question of narrativity; in other words, the extent to which history itself is already a story-shaped phenomenon, even before the historian begins to reconstruct it as a followable story. With such major discussions taking place, I argued that a purely text-immanent approach to John's narrative art was dangerously limited and even reductionist. Narrative critics, I contended, need to ask deeper questions concerning the relationship between history and narrative in the gospel. To be sure we need a better understanding of the surface, narrative qualities of the text and this is the right place to begin the process of interpretation, as Culpepper showed. But a purely synchronic method will only tell half the story. Narrative criticism must offer a more integrated hermeneutic.

In what follows I would therefore like to provide the reader with a study of the style of John 11.1–44, the story of the raising of Lazarus. I will use the narrative-critical approach which I introduced in *John as Storyteller*, an approach which takes into account both the literary and the historical issues which the text raises. Building on the study of this text in my narrative-critical commentary on John (Stibbe 1993a), and on an article entitled 'A Tomb with A View' published in *New Testament Studies* (1994), I would like to attempt an analysis of John's narrative style which pays close attention to the final form of the narrative, as well as the sources behind it.

JOHN 11.1–44

In 1923, Hans Windisch described John 11.1–44 as 'a family novella, full of moving human features, like the story of the prodigal son, or even better the Tobit narrative'. He called it 'a dramatically formed *family novella*: three siblings – two sisters, the brother terminally ill; they send for the family friend, the miracle doctor; he comes too late' (cited in Stibbe 1993b: 37). Though I will question the use of 'novella' as an apt description of the form of this story, Windisch's lucid prose does depict the emotive appeal of what may well be the finest narrative in the New Testament. In the NIV, the story goes as follows:

> Now a man named Lazarus was sick. He was from Bethany, the village of Mary and her sister Martha. ²This Mary, whose brother Lazarus now lay sick, was the same one who poured perfume on the Lord and wiped his feet with her hair. ³So the sisters sent word to Jesus, 'Lord, the one you love is sick'.
> ⁴When he heard this, Jesus said, 'This sickness will not end in death. No, it is for God's glory so that God's Son may be glorified through it'. ⁵Jesus loved Martha and her sister and Lazarus. ⁶Yet when he heard that Lazarus was sick, he stayed where he was two more days.
> ⁷Then he said to his disciples, 'Let us go back to Judea'.
> ⁸'But Rabbi,' they said, 'a short while ago the Jews tried to stone you, and yet you are going back there?'
> ⁹Jesus answered, 'Are there not twelve hours of daylight? A

man who walks by day will not stumble, for he sees by this world's light. [10]It is when he walks by night that he stumbles, for he has no light.'

[11]After he had said this, he went on to tell them, 'Our friend Lazarus has fallen asleep; but I am going there to wake him up'.

[12]His disciples replied, 'Lord, if he sleeps, he will get better'. [13]Jesus had been speaking of his death, but his disciples thought he meant natural sleep.

[14]So then he told them plainly, 'Lazarus is dead, [15]and for your sake I am glad I was not there, so that you may believe. But let us go to him'.

[16]Then Thomas (called Didymus) said to the rest of the disciples, 'Let us also go, that we may die with him'.

[17]On his arrival, Jesus found that Lazarus had already been in the tomb for four days. [18]Bethany was less than two miles from Jerusalem, [19]and many Jews had come to Martha and Mary to comfort them in the loss of their brother. [20]When Martha heard that Jesus was coming, she went out to meet him, but Mary stayed at home.

[21]'Lord', Martha said to Jesus, 'if you had been here, my brother would not have died. [22]But I know that even now God will give you whatever you ask'.

[23]Jesus said to her, 'Your brother will rise again'.

[24]Martha answered, 'I know that he will rise again in the resurrection at the last day'.

[25]Jesus said to her, 'I am the resurrection and the life. He who believes in me will live, even though he dies; [26]and whoever lives and believes in me will never die. Do you believe this?'

[27]'Yes, Lord', she told him, 'I believe that you are the Christ, the Son of God, who was to come into the world'.

[28]And after she had said this, she went back and called her sister Mary aside. 'The Teacher is here', she said, 'and is asking for you'. [29]When Mary heard this, she got up quickly and went to him. [30]Now Jesus had not yet entered the village but was still at the place where Martha had met him. [31]When the Jews who had been with Mary in the house, comforting her, noticed how quickly she got up and went out, they followed her, supposing she was going to the tomb to mourn there.

[32]When Mary reached the place where Jesus was and saw him, she fell at his feet and said, 'Lord, if you had been here, my brother would not have died'.

³³When Jesus saw her weeping, and the Jews who had come along with her also weeping, he was deeply moved in spirit and troubled. ³⁴'Where have you laid him?' he asked.

'Come and see, Lord', they replied.

³⁵Jesus wept.

³⁶Then the Jews said, 'See how he loved him'.

³⁷But some of them said, 'Could not he who opened the eyes of the blind man have kept this man from dying?'

³⁸Jesus, once more deeply moved, came to the tomb. It was a cave with a stone laid across the entrance. ³⁹'Take away the stone', he said.

'But Lord,' said Martha, the sister of the dead man, 'by this time there is a bad odour, for he has been there four days'.

⁴⁰Then Jesus said, 'Did I not tell you that if you believed, you would see the glory of God?'

⁴¹So they took away the stone. Then Jesus looked up and said, 'Father, I thank you that you have heard me. ⁴²I knew that you always hear me, but I said this for the benefit of the people standing here, that they may believe that you sent me'.

⁴³When he had said this, Jesus called in a loud voice, 'Lazarus, come out!' ⁴⁴The dead man came out, his hands and feet wrapped with strips of linen, and a cloth around his face.

Jesus said to them, 'Take off the grave clothes, and let him go'.

CONTEXT

Narrative criticism begins with a detailed consideration of the context of a story. No story in a gospel like John is to be studied in isolation. It is part of the plot of the whole gospel and must therefore be placed within the overall flow of the evolving drama.

What is immediately visible is the pivotal nature of John 11.1–44. The plot of the gospel thus far has moved through definable stages. In John 1, the narrator introduces Jesus of Nazareth in the most exalted terms. In John 2.1–4.54, the narrator depicts a journey from Cana in Galilee (where Jesus turns the water into wine), through Jerusalem (where Jesus cleanses the temple and dialogues with Nicodemus), through Perea (where the Baptist witnesses to the superiority of Jesus) and Samaria (the story of the woman at the well) back to Cana in Galilee (where Jesus heals the royal official's little boy). In this phase Jesus performs his ministry without discernible hostility from anyone.

In the next phase of the gospel, extending from John 5.1 to John 10.42, Jesus begins a second itinerary. He begins in Jerusalem with the healing of the crippled man at the pool of Bethesda, a miracle which engenders intense antipathy from the Jewish authorities (John 5). He then travels to Galilee where he performs several miracles (the feeding of the five thousand and the walking on the sea) before teaching in the synagogue in Capernaum, where a heated debate takes place concerning 'bread from heaven' (John 6). Jesus then travels back to Jerusalem for the feast of Tabernacles where his Messianic status and his heavenly paternity are disputed, and where his life is again threatened by the Jewish hierarchy (John 7–8). He goes into hiding (John 8.59) but then immediately reappears to heal a man born blind (John 9), an action which elicits further opposition from the Jewish leaders at the Feast of Dedication (John 10). By the time we come to John 11, Jesus' hour (the time of his death and departure) seems to be very imminent. Indeed, the reader is given the clear impression that it will only be one more controversy which will lead to Jesus' arrest.

John 11–12 depicts a key *peripeteia* or turning point in the plot of the gospel. At the beginning of John 11, Jesus begins the final earthly journey of his ministry with his pilgrimage to Jerusalem for the final Passover of his life. The event which precipitates this journey is the death of one whom Jesus is said specifically to love – a man who has hitherto not been introduced. His name is Lazarus. He lives just outside Jerusalem in a village called Bethany, and his sisters (Martha and Mary) send word to Jesus that their brother is ill. Jesus arrives too late; Lazarus has already died and has been in the family tomb for four days. Jesus however performs what is unquestionably the most spectacular miracle in the gospel and raises Lazarus from death. Lazarus emerges from the tomb still wrapped in his grave clothes.

This miracle proves to be the final straw for the Jerusalem authorities. They meet with Caiaphas in John 11.45ff and decide that there is now a real danger of a strong Jesus movement which will threaten the status quo in Palestine. Knowing that the Romans may regard Jesus and his disciples as a political threat, Caiaphas and the Sanhedrin make a decision that Jesus must die. The rest of John 11 and John 12 describes their search for Jesus, and subsequently Jesus' triumphal entry into Jerusalem. Jesus' open movements now seal his fate. He has apparently played into the hands of his enemies. It can now only be a matter of time before Jesus is arrested, tried and executed.

As far as context is concerned, the raising of Lazarus therefore occupies a critical position in the plot of the gospel. It is the raising of Lazarus which secures Jesus' fate. In Mark, Matthew and Luke, the cleansing of the temple is the event which brings the authorities to boiling point. In John, the cleansing of the temple occurs as early as Chapter 2 and it is now the Lazarus episode which occupies this key position in the plot. It is therefore probable that the narrative depicting the cleansing of the temple was, in the last stages of John's composition, moved to the beginning of the gospel. The Lazarus episode was then used to fill the gap. As we will see in the section on characterization, in historical terms this highlights the importance of Lazarus and his two sisters in the community for which the gospel was written. For the moment, however, the reader should note the startling paradox which the author creates by placing the Lazarus episode at this point. *It is the act of giving life to Lazarus which leads to Jesus' death.*

FORM

From context it is always wise to move to the literary form of a narrative. In the case of the Lazarus episode, it takes no great scholarship to identify John 11.1–44 as a miracle story. The miracle story is a recognizable literary form in both John and the Synoptics. Indeed, there are seven miracle stories in John 1–12: the transformation of water into wine (John 2.1–11), the healing of the royal official's son (John 4.46–54), the healing of the crippled man (John 5.1–15), the feeding of the five thousand (John 6.1–15), the miraculous sea-crossing (John 6.16–21), the healing of the man born blind (John 9), and the raising of Lazarus (John 11.1–44). We should recall that seven was regarded by Jews as a number symbolizing completeness or perfection. As I pointed out in Chapter 1, by making the Lazarus narrative the seventh miracle in the gospel, the author suggests that it is this event which is the most dramatic and the most perfect of Jesus' miraculous works. No other charismatic sign is quite like this one.

Further investigation bears this out. There is a uniqueness about this narrative in formal terms. In my previous research into the miracle stories in John's gospel, I identified four different miracle traditions behind John's gospel. I proposed that there was first of all a signs source. The two stories from this source are both called 'signs', they both occur in Cana, and they both have the same essential structure. I am referring to the wine miracle in John 2.1–11 and the healing miracle in John 4.46–54. These are very similar to one another. In both, a request is made to Jesus (by Jesus' mother in John 2 and by the royal official in John 4). In both Jesus rebukes the requester. In both Jesus responds with a miraculous work in spite of his rebuke. Both, in other words, follow the same pattern. I concluded that the presence of this foundational structure of a request, a rebuke and a response in both narratives is precisely the kind of feature one would expect to find in stories emanating from the same oral tradition.

If the first miracle tradition can legitimately be described as a Cana signs source, the second can legitimately be described as a Galilean sea source. Three miracles recorded in John's gospel come from this source: the feeding of the five thousand in John 6.1–15, which occurs by the Sea of Galilee; the miraculous crossing of the Galilean Sea in John 6.16–21, which was connected to the multiplication miracle at the earliest stages (see Mark 6.30–44, 6.45–52); and the fishing miracle recorded in John 21.1–15, which has obvious parallels with John 6.1–15 (see the distribution of bread and fish in John 21.13). These three stories are so markedly different from those which I attributed to the signs source that I concluded that they must be derived from a distinctive catena of Galilean Sea miracles.

The third miracle tradition which I claimed to discern was a catena of Jerusalem 'pool' miracles. The first of these is recorded in John 5.1–15. It involves the healing of a poor and marginalized Jew in a pool (Bethesda) on the sabbath, and it leads to a legal investigation. The second of these is recorded in John 9. This story involves the healing of a poor and marginalised Jew in a pool (Siloam) on the sabbath, and also leads to a legal investigation. Here again we are dealing with two stories with remarkable similarities. They are the furthest remove from those which the author drew from the signs source. The signs were in Galilee, these are in Jerusalem. The signs had an aristocratic ethos (the feast at Cana and the royal official from Capernaum), these involve the *Am ha-aretz* (the poor). Furthermore, these Jerusalem pool miracles are overtly different from the Galilean Sea miracles. The sea miracles occur in the country; the pool miracles occur in the city. The sea miracles do not lead to any kind of forensic process; the pool miracles lead to informal trials.

An overview of my research therefore looks like this:

Miracle Traditions in the Fourth Gospel

Group A   The Cana signs source (×2)

Group B   The Galilean Sea miracles (×3)

Group C   The Jerusalem pool miracles (×2)

From these three traditions, the author selected, interpreted and redescribed two and at the most three examples. That he could have selected many more is indicated by the narrator's confession in John 20.31: 'Jesus did many other miraculous signs in the presence of his disciples, which are not recorded in this book'. A similar note is struck in the narrator's final comments 'au lecteur' in John 21.25: 'Jesus did many other things as well. If every one of them were written down, I suppose that even the whole world would not have room for the books that would be written'.

This source-critical probe throws into relief the formal distinctiveness of the Lazarus episode in John 11.1–44. There are no obvious correspondences with the three sets of narratives mentioned above. The raising of Lazarus does not occur at the sea of Galilee, nor does it take place on the sabbath in a pool in Jerusalem. It is possible to argue that there are some very vague similarities with the Cana miracles. In John 11.1–44, there does seem to be a case to be made for a request–rebuke–response pattern, insofar as the sisters request Jesus' help, Jesus delays and rebukes the disciples, before responding with a dramatic miracle. However, it is nothing like as clear as the much shorter narratives in John 2.1–11 and John 4.46–54, and the reader should note that Jesus does not rebuke the requester (the sisters) and that the setting is outside Jerusalem (the south) not in Cana (the north).

Furthermore, the plot of the Lazarus episode is utterly distinctive. In all the other miracle stories in John's gospel, the actual miracle occurs either at the beginning or at the mid-point of the plot. In John 11.1–44, however, the miracle occurs at the end of the narrative, with Jesus' climactic pronouncement, 'Lazarus, come out!' (11.43). Finally, we need to stress the obvious point that John 11.1–44 is the only example of a resurrection miracle in the fourth gospel. Again this reveals the formal distinctiveness of the Lazarus episode. Here we are dealing with material from a fourth miracle tradition: one with no recognizable formula. Far from being a 'family novella', John 11.1–44 is the only example of a resurrection miracle story in the fourth gospel.

The literary form of the Lazarus narrative is therefore unique in many respects, as the following table shows:

Miracle	Text	Formal similarities with other miracles
The first sign at Cana	2.1–11	4.46–54. Request–rebuke–response structure, Setting in Cana, description as *semeion* (sign).
The second sign at Cana	4.46–54	2.1–11. Request–rebuke–response structure, Setting in Cana, description as *semeion*.
The healing of the crippled man	5.1–15	9.1–41. Setting in Jerusalem, pool – followed by trial scene, etc.
The feeding of the 5,000	6.1–15	6.16–21. The setting (Sea of Galilee) and context (6.1–15 and 6.16–21 are juxtaposed)
The crossing of the sea	6.16–21	6.1–15. The setting (Sea of Galilee) and context (6.16–21 follows directly after 6.1–15)
The healing of the man born blind	ch.9	5.1–15. Setting in Jerusalem, pool – followed by trial scene, etc.
The raising of Lazarus	11.1–44	No obvious parallels

PLOT

I have already begun a discussion concerning the plot of the Lazarus episode in my comments above on the form of this narrative. The most distinctive feature of the plot, in formal terms, is that the miracle does not come at the beginning or the middle of the story, but at its conclusion. No other miracle story in John delays the actual miracle in this way.

Already, then, I have begun to make some remarks about the three stages which are characteristic of 'plots': the beginning, the middle, and the end. One of the features which is most noticeable about John 11.1–44 is the way in which the author has arranged his material so clearly into three such phases of action and place. The first phase of action occurs in John 11.1–16 where Jesus is depicted as 'outside Judea'. That this is the setting becomes apparent in v.7 where Jesus says, 'Let us go back to Judea'. In this first phase, therefore, the action takes place outside Judea, and consists of a request sent to Jesus from the sisters of Lazarus, and the reaction of Jesus and his disciples to this request.

In v.17, a second phase of action and place is initiated. Between v.16 and v.17, a journey to Bethany (Lazarus' home) is implied but not stated. As so often in John, this is a gap which the reader has to fill. From vv.17–37 we have the longest phase of the narrative. This occurs outside the village and involves two dialogues, one between Jesus and Martha, and another between Jesus and Mary. That this occurs outside Bethany is made clear by the narrator in v.30, where we read that 'Jesus had not yet entered the village, but was still at the place where Martha had met him'.

A third and final phase is begun in v.38 and extends to v.44. Here the action takes place outside the tomb where Lazarus' body has been laid. In v.38 the narrator simply states that 'Jesus came to the tomb', and then describes the setting in more detail: 'It was a cave with a stone laid across the entrance'. In this final phase, Jesus prays to the Father and then performs the miracle. Lazarus emerges from the tomb alive.

Looking at the beginning, the middle and the end of the Lazarus narrative, the following plot sequence is therefore discernible:

Beginning: Jesus is told of Lazarus' illness but delays his journey to Bethany (vv.1–16).

Middle: Jesus arrives at Bethany and speaks with Martha and Mary outside the village (vv.17–37).

End: Jesus comes to the tomb and raises Lazarus from the dead (vv.38–44).

The feature which enables us to discern this sequence is the creative use of settings. In phase 1 we are 'outside Judea'. In phase 2 we are 'outside Bethany'. In phase 3 we are 'outside the tomb'. There is, in other words, a gradual 'homing in' on the tomb of Lazarus through the careful use of focalization. In terms of geographical setting, we move from a very wide-angled focus ('outside Judea') to a very precise focus ('outside the tomb'). It is John's sense of place which leads to this demarcation of the plot into three phases:

$$\begin{array}{ccccc} \text{Outside Judea} & \rightarrow & \text{Outside Bethany} & \rightarrow & \text{Outside the tomb} \\ \text{vv.1–16} & & \text{vv.17–37} & & \text{vv.38–44} \end{array}$$

TIME

From this brief analysis we can see that there is evidence of conscious and careful plotting of material in John 11.1–44. This is further highlighted by the way in which the narrator uses 'time' in the Lazarus episode. As I showed in Chapter 2, authors create plots by arranging material temporally as well as causally. It is the temporal structure of John 11.1–44 which interests us here.

What emerges as we examine John's use of time in this narrative is the huge disparity between John 11.11–16 and John 11.17–44. The first phase of the story involves a period of several days (11.1–16). We know this because the sisters send word to Jesus that Lazarus is ill in vv.1–3, he delays his return by two more days, and when he does arrive at Bethany, he finds that Lazarus has been in the tomb for four days. This means that we must assume a minimum of three days in story time between the beginning of phase one and the beginning of phase two.

The story time of phases two and three, however, involves only a period of minutes. The time which it takes for Jesus to move from outside the village to the entrance of the tomb is not specified. However, one gets the distinct impression that narrative time (the time it takes to read the story) and the story time (the process of time depicted in the story) are one and the same. We are, in other words, watching the miracle as it happened.

Thus there is a substantial temporal imbalance between the first phase of the narrative, and the second and third phases. Phase one takes a minimum of two days. Phases two and three take a maximum of a few minutes. Why is this?

The commentaries all provide one obvious answer to this question. They point out that Jews at this time believed that the soul hovered over a body for four days after death, and that on the fourth day it departed. The fourth day was therefore the critical day. It was on this day that a person could be said to be truly dead. By delaying Jesus' return to Judea for four days, the narrator manages implicitly to inform the reader that Lazarus is unquestionably dead. His soul has now departed. Resurrecting Lazarus would therefore be a great miracle. It would involve the reunification of his soul with his body!

The temporal imbalance in the Lazarus episode therefore has a lot to do with the Jewish understanding of death. But this may not be the only reason. There may well be another, more artistic motivation at work here as well. To detect this aesthetic impulse, the reader should note the temporal imbalance in the plot of the gospel as a whole. The first half of John's gospel (Chapters 1–12) depicts a period of between two and three years. The second half (Chapters 13–21) depicts a period of under two weeks. It may be that the author of John 11.1–44 is trying to create a similarity between the use of time in John 11.1–44, and the use of time in the fourth gospel as a whole. It may be that something of the overall plot-shape of the gospel is consciously imitated in the temporal emplotment of the Lazarus episode. The part, in short, reflects the whole.

DEEP STRUCTURE

This is further borne out if we expose the Lazarus narrative to the kind of actantial, structuralist analysis which I described in Chapter 2. Using Greimas' terminology, we can see that the Sender figures in the story are the two sisters Mary and Martha, who literally send for Jesus (*apesteilan*, v.3, from *apostello*, 'I send'). Jesus is therefore the Receiver of the commission, and the object of the narrative 'commission' given to him is to bring health to Lazarus.

The opponent of Jesus in the story is not easy to discover. The Jews are remarkably non-confrontational in 11.1–44 and even seem to participate with sincerity in the mourning process. From the reaction of Jesus outside the tomb, however – where he is visibly troubled and even 'angry' – it would appear that the Opponent pole of the narrative is not a person but rather that which has destroyed Lazarus and saddened his loved ones, namely 'death'. Death is Jesus' enemy in John 11.1–44.

The Helper figure in the narrative is also unclear. The mourners help Jesus to find the tomb but they do not help him to perform the miracle. The Father could be said to be Jesus' helper, and yet the prayer which Jesus prays seems to be for the benefit of the bystanders, and not a request for help: 'Father, I thank you that you have heard me. I knew that you always hear me, but I said this for the benefit of the people standing here, that they may believe you sent me'. As in John 17, this kind of prayer looks more like a revelation (for the benefit of the bystanders) than a supplication (for divine assistance).

As far as the Subject of the story is concerned, this is clearly Jesus. The Object is the raising of Lazarus; the restoration of life to one who has died.

In diagrammatic form, the deep plot-structure of John 11.1–44 therefore looks like this:

Sender (Mary/Martha)	Object (life/health)	Receiver (Jesus)
axis of communication		
	axis of volition	
axis of power		
Helper (none?)	Subject (Jesus)	Opponent (Death)

Put in this way, we can see again how John 11.1–44 is a kind of microcosm of the whole gospel. From this actantial overview it has become apparent that the deep plot-structure of John 11.1–44 has fundamental parallels with the deep plot-structure of the gospel as a whole (see Chapter 2). In John's gospel Jesus is also one sent. He is also a man without Helpers. The object of his mission is also to bring life into a world of sin and death. All these features are repeated *in miniature* in the Lazarus episode. John 11.1–44 contains within it something of the shape and character of the whole gospel.

MODE

A final indication of this sense of 'hologrammatic' conformity (the part imitating the whole) is the way in which the generic mode of the Lazarus narrative reflects the generic mode of the whole gospel. The gospel as a whole has a U-shaped plot. It begins on a comic and romantic note (John 2–4), proceeds into a satirical phase (John 5–10), then on into a tragic sequence (the farewell of Jesus and his death in John 13–19) before returning to the comic and even romantic note with which we started (the resurrection in John 20–21). In Northrop Frye's terminology, the U-shaped plot of the gospel represents the *mythos* of spring – a *mythos* which, in its simplest form, depicts a descent from freedom into bondage, and then an ascent from bondage to freedom.

John's use of this comic mode is actually very appropriate. The Johannine picture of the journey of the Word is fundamentally U-shaped as well. Jesus-the-Word descends to earth, is made flesh, is baptized in his thirties, ministers for a period of about three years, before dying on a Roman cross. This death is seen as part of Jesus' ascent. It is a lifting up. It is, like the resurrection, part of the journey home. In creating a plot for his gospel, John therefore *inevitably* resorts to the comic mode of representation. The U-shaped journey of the Word requires a U-shaped *mythos*.

The Lazarus episode has the same comic *mythos* as the whole gospel. If we begin in 10.40–42, we can see that the story begins on a very high note as far as Jesus' ministry is concerned. Here the narrator reports that many believed in Jesus. Subsequently, there is a sense of descent into something far darker, more tragic indeed, as Jesus returns to the place of great danger (Judea) to weep over his friend's death. However, the story ends with a definite ascent into the comic (often signalled by the theme of resurrection) as Jesus raises Lazarus and many are said, once again, to believe in him (11.45). The use of this comic mode, like John's use of time and deep structure, reinforces the sense that John 11.1–44 is a microcosm of the gospel in its entirety.

PROLEPSES

If John is consciously telling the story of Lazarus in a way which is supposed to resonate with the gospel as a whole, then we would expect to find some prolepses or 'flash-forwards' which link the death and resurrection of Lazarus to the death and resurrection of Jesus. This is precisely what we do find.

There is, first of all, an ironic prolepsis of the passion in John 11.1–44. Notice the narrator's use of *ekraugasen* ('called out') in v.42: 'Jesus called in a loud voice, "Lazarus, come out!"' This reference to Jesus shouting is a 'flash-forward' to the passion, where the same word is used for the persistent shouting of the Jews for Jesus' death. In 18.40, the Jews are said to shout out (*ekraugasan*), 'Give us Barabbas!'. In 19.6, we read that the chief priests and the officials see Jesus before Pilate. The narrator says, 'They shouted (*ekraugasan*), "Crucify him! Crucify him!"' In 19.12, Pilate tries to set Jesus free but is thwarted because, according to the narrator, 'the Jews kept on shouting (*ekraugasan*)'. In 19.15, Pilate tells the Jews, 'Here is your king!'. But 'they shouted' (*ekraugasan*), 'We have no king but Caesar!' These four shouts for death are intended by the reader as an ironic contrast with Jesus' shout for life in 11.42. They link the death of Lazarus with the death of Jesus.

But there are, secondly, prolepses of the resurrection of Jesus in the Lazarus episode. When Lazarus emerges from the tomb wrapped with strips of linen and a cloth around his face (*soudarion*, John 11.44), the person rereading the gospel is supposed to see in this an anticipation of the empty tomb in John 20. In John 20.7, Simon Peter peers into the empty tomb and sees the head-cloth (*soudarion*) of Jesus lying there. John 11.44 and John 20.7 contain the only references to grave clothes (with specific reference to the *soudarion*) in the fourth gospel. Furthermore, the reader should note the echoes between the conduct of Jesus at the tomb of Lazarus and the conduct of Mary Magdalene at the tomb of Jesus in John 20. Mary, like Jesus, weeps at the tomb in 20.11 (compare 11.35). Mary, like Jesus, is concerned to know where the body is laid (20.13, 15 – compare 11.34). The raising of Lazarus is therefore linked to the raising of Jesus through the subtle use of echo effects. Again, as far as John 11.1–44 is concerned, the Lazarus episode can be regarded as a microcosm of the whole gospel.

NARRATOR

These remarks highlight the extraordinary complexity of the role of the narrator in the Lazarus episode. To be sure, there are many aspects of the narrator's role which are simple and conventional. It is the narrator who informs us of the identity of speakers, the movements of Jesus, the relationships between characters, the issues which are foundational to the story, various actions, details of setting, the emotions and thoughts of those involved, explanatory asides, and so forth. In these and other matters, the role of the narrator is pervasive but straightforward.

However, the way in which the author uses the narrator to link the Lazarus episode with other parts of the gospel is less simple. If our discussion of prolepses has shown anything, it has revealed how John's story has been constructed for rereading. This fact is indicated by the curious remark by the narrator in 11.2, that 'this Mary, whose brother Lazarus now lay sick, was the same one who poured perfume on the Lord and wiped his feet with her hair'. Here the game is given away. First-time readers will be mystified by this comment. They will interpret it as an analepsis (a flash-back) of something which has already occurred. In vain they will search the previous chapters for a scene in which Mary of Bethany anoints the feet of Jesus. Giving up, they will read on and find the relevant episode in the next chapter, indeed at the very start of ch.12! What the first-time reader interprets as a flash-back is really a flash-forward. Put another way, the narrator makes an analeptic reference to an event which is really proleptic.

There is therefore something rather curious and complex about the narrator in the fourth gospel. Indeed, like the protagonist, the narrator is a somewhat elusive character, making constant demands on the reader and requiring energetic perseverence as far as correct understanding is concerned. Above all, the narrator tells the story in such a way that it is only by rereading it that the interconnectedness of the parts of the gospel can be appreciated. In this strategy, the end of the story is of particular importance. The death and resurrection of Jesus (John 18–20) must be constantly kept in mind if the reader is to discover the deeper nuances in the multi-story texture of the narrative. Such readers will only hear the quiet whisperings of the narrator if they read the gospel from the perspective of its concluding denouement. Only those who already have the shouting of the mob in John 18–19 at the back of their minds will discern the paradox in Jesus' shout for life in John 11.43. Only those who already have the grave clothes of Jesus in the back of their minds will discern the significance of Lazarus' grave clothes in John 11.44.

The narrator therefore has a particular kind of reader in view: one who follows the beginning and the middle of the story always from the point of view of its end. In this respect, narrative form and Christological claim are inseparable, for it is one of the fundamental claims of the fourth gospel that the end of history (the eschaton) has appeared ahead of time in the person of Jesus. Privileges reserved for Yahweh on the last day (such as raising the dead, judgement, eternal life) are portrayed by John as being dispensed during the ministry of Jesus right now. John's eschatology (understanding of the last things) is therefore primarily a realized eschatology not a future eschatology, and his Christology is one which stresses that Jesus is the revealer and mediator of the *eschata* (last things). Indeed, the raising of Lazarus is perhaps the most spectacular demonstration of this, for as Jesus claims in John 5.25: 'I tell you the truth, a time is coming *and has now come* when the dead will hear the voice of the Son of God and those who hear will live' [my emphasis].

As far as the narrative form of the gospel is concerned, we need to recognize that the narrator relates to readers whose response is a matter of *realized eschatology*; that is, a matter of living in the end-time of the story even while it is still in progress. Readers of John 11.1–44 need, to some extent, to interpret this miracle in the light of the greatest of all signs, the death and resurrection of Jesus. They need to read the story in the light of its ending. As such, narrative form and Christological claim are inseparable. For in the content of the story Jesus Christ is depicted as the eschaton-in-person, the one who brings the end of history into the middle of time.

PROTAGONIST

All this brings us to a long overdue discussion of characterization in the Lazarus episode, and specifically to an appreciation of the way in which Jesus is portrayed.

There are a number of features which are worthy of mention. First of all, we need to underline the point which has already been made implicitly that Jesus is depicted as the incarnation of God, as Yahweh in human form. Jesus raises Lazarus from the dead, an act which was associated with Yahweh on the last day of history. Jesus uses the phrase 'I am' in his pronouncement, 'I am the resurrection and the life' (John 11.25). 'I am' is *ego eimi* in Greek, and *ego eimi* is used in Deutero Isaiah (Isaiah 40–55) as a form of Yahweh's name. Jesus is therefore using a formula of divine revelation in this story. Furthermore, the 'I am' saying in 11.25 constitutes an overt claim on Jesus' part to be the eschaton-in-person. Martha has just said that she knows that Lazarus will rise *on the last day* (11.24). Now, in 11.25, Jesus says that he himself is that eschatological hope. He is the resurrection. He is the life. So whatever else may be said about Jesus in John 11.1–44, his divinity is unmistakable. At the tomb of Lazarus is one who is so close to God that he can use Yahweh's name, speak Yahweh's words, and perform Yahweh's actions.

This primary characteristic of Jesus in John 11.1–44 should not, however, obscure a second important aspect – namely, evidence of Jesus' humanity. Though hard and fast distinctions between what is divine and what is human are not straightforward, we ought to notice certain 'human' traits to which the narrator draws our attention. These figure in vv.33–35 when Jesus hears the poignant cries of Mary and her fellow mourners. As he does so, the narrator provides a rare glimpse into the emotions of Jesus. We are told in v.33 that 'When Jesus saw her weeping, and the Jews who had come along with her also weeping, he was deeply moved in spirit and troubled'. The verb translated as 'deeply moved' is *embrimasthai* which denotes anger. The phrase 'in spirit' is *en pneumati* which indicates that this anger is given internal but not external expression (Barrett 1978: 398–9). By describing Jesus as 'deeply moved in spirit', the narrator affords us a rare insight into Jesus' emotions. As Jesus sees the grief all around him, he becomes angry about the suffering caused by death. The narrator's words here suggest an inner rage at the work of Satan.

This profound anger in the context of bereavement is a thoroughly human reaction. So is the second feature mentioned in v.33. The narrator says not only that Jesus was 'deeply moved in spirit' but also that he was 'troubled'. The Greek verb is *tarassein* which is used in a psychological sense in John 14.1 and John 14.27 where Jesus says to his disciples, 'Do not let your hearts be troubled (*tarassein*)'. In John 14, Jesus is referring to the fearful anxiety which the disciples may experience when they themselves are bereaved; in other words, when they witness the death of Jesus. In John 12.27, Jesus himself experiences this anxiety as he contemplates his own death. There Jesus declares, 'Now my heart is troubled' (*tarassein*). In John 13.21, Jesus experiences the same emotion as he speaks of his betrayal by Judas. There the narrator uses *tarassein* again and informs us that 'Jesus was troubled in spirit' (note the addition of *to pneumati*). When the narrator says in 11.33 that Jesus was troubled it can only mean that Jesus so identified with the bereaved that he himself shared that deep-seated existential anxiety which is felt in the face of death.

The note of sympathy struck in 11.33 is extremely important. It reveals that Jesus is a deity who enters into the suffering of humanity. He is not some gnostic phantom who stands aloof from human pain. He does not conduct his ministry in a state of Platonic *apatheia* (remoteness). Rather, Jesus feels what the mourners feel. He is deeply angered in his spirit and experiences that chill of mortal anxiety which they have sensed around the tomb of Lazarus. Furthermore, in v.35 the narrator tells us that 'Jesus wept'. The verb for 'wept' is *dakruein* which is different from the word used so far of Mary and the mourners (*klaiein*). It is used in the aorist and has the sense of bursting into tears. 'Jesus wept' would therefore be better translated, 'Jesus burst into tears'. At the sight of Mary's grief, and the mourning of those around her, Jesus participates in the fullest and most authentic way in the emotions of the bystanders. Indeed, the use of *dakruein* rather than *klaiein* may even suggest that he entered *more* fully into that grief.

The characterization of Jesus in John 11.1–44 therefore advances the discussion of both Jesus' divinity and his humanity. Above all, it greatly assists us in any discussion of the incarnation, of the participation of the Word of God in our humanity. We have already seen Jesus' readiness to enter into the major rites of passage which human beings face. The first miracle in the gospel records Jesus' full involvement in a wedding at Cana. There the atmosphere was festive. Now, in the seventh miracle, Jesus is portrayed as one fully involved at the scene of Lazarus' burial. Here the atmosphere is funereal. At a marriage and a death, the Johannine Jesus is revealed to be the Messiah who is prepared to enter into all of our limit-situations.

Do such positive characteristics encourage us to identify with Jesus and regard his portrayal in a sympathetic light? To a degree they must do. The sight of Jesus entering into the oldest fear of all (that of death), and entering into the two most common emotions of bereaved people (grief and anger) can only evoke a sense of solidarity between contemporary readers and the protagonist of John 11.1–44. Here John seems to be presenting a narrative theodicy which has much to offer the sick, the suffering and the dying. This is a Saviour who weeps when we weep and feels what we feel.

At the same time, however, we ought to note the way the author continues to suggest a note of aloofness in Jesus' character. In Chapter 1 I described the primary characteristic of the Johannine Jesus as 'elusiveness'. This elusiveness is particularly focused in Jesus' actions and speech, and again we see precisely this in the Lazarus episode. Notice the way in which Jesus delays his return to Bethany after being sent such a desperate and urgent message for help. Here Jesus' actions are elusive in the extreme. He will not conform to human timetables (John 7.6).

If Jesus' actions are elusive, so is his speech. We should note in particular two very enigmatic sayings. The first is in vv.9–10: 'Are there not twelve hours of daylight? A man who walks by day will not stumble, for he sees by the world's light. It is when he walks by night that he stumbles, for he has no light.' As so often, Jesus' words are patient of both a literal and a symbolic interpretation. At the literal level, Jesus is simply saying (paraphrased), 'During the hours of daylight, one's movements can be free and unhampered. When darkness sets in, however, one must be more cautious. The lack of light could cause one to fall.' At the metaphorical level, these same words can be paraphrased thus: 'I am the light of the world. So long as men walk with me they will see the way. But those who live without me live in darkness and will find me a stumbling block. They will surely fall.'

Jesus' words to his disciples in 11.1–16 are therefore elusive. He utters a *mashal* in vv.9–10 which is far from clear. Indeed, it is not until v.14 that he starts to speak to them 'plainly'. The adverb translated 'plainly' is *parresia* which is a keyword in John's portrayal of the elusive Christ. In relation to Jesus' movements it refers to open and public action. Thus, Jesus' brothers encourage him to go publicly (*parresia*) to Jerusalem (7.10). In relation to Jesus' words *parresia* refers to plain meaning. Thus, Jesus' disciples exclaim in John 16.29 that Jesus is at last speaking 'plainly' (*parresia*) and not 'in riddles' (*en paroimiais*). Here in John 11.9–10, the disciples might have justly complained that Jesus was not speaking plainly but in riddles!

So there is a certain aloofness in Jesus' words to the disciples in phase one of the Lazarus episode. There is also a certain elusiveness in the second enigmatic saying of Jesus, this time in conversation with Martha in John 11.25–26. Here the language of Jesus moves without warning from the literal to the spiritual and back again, so that only the perceptive reader penetrates the complete meaning of what is said: 'I am the resurrection and the life. He who believes in me will live (spiritually), even though he dies (physically); and whoever lives (physically) and believes in me will never die (spiritually)'. The whole saying depends upon the reader's ability to discern the following chiasmus:

$$a^1 \text{ Life (spiritual)} \qquad b^1 \text{ death (physical)}$$
$$b^2 \text{ death (spiritual)} \qquad a^2 \text{ life (physical)}$$

It is impossible to discern just how fully Martha grasps this complex pronouncement.

As far as John's portrayal of Jesus is concerned, we must conclude that in the Lazarus episode the protagonist has features which attract the reader (a Christology of human solidarity) and at the same time features which keep Jesus beyond our full apprehension and comprehension (his elusive action and speech). Jesus is therefore a complex character in John 11.1–44. On the one hand he can weep with compassion (v.35). On the other he can say, 'I am glad I was not there' (v.15).

MINOR CHARACTERS

Whilst Jesus is, as always in John, the focus of attention, there are a number of minor characters in the dramatis personae of the Lazarus episode. These are used as 'foils'. In other words, they are employed by the author as a means by which traits of the protagonist can be highlighted for the reader.

In phase 1 of the plot, the minor characters who are actually present with Jesus are known as 'the disciples'. They are not introduced until v.7, but it can be presumed that Jesus is speaking to them in vv.4–6. These disciples are portrayed as an anxious, rather otiose group. They object to Jesus wanting to go back to Judea because they know that he is likely to be assassinated there (v.8). They fail to understand what Jesus is saying in v.11 when Jesus says that Lazarus is asleep. They take 'sleep' literally and argue that Lazarus will get better if he sleeps. The narrator points out in an aside (a common literary device) that they had completely misunderstood Jesus: 'Jesus had been speaking of Lazarus' death, but his disciples thought he meant natural sleep' (v.13). This shows that the disciples in John 11 are solely introduced in order to highlight Jesus' knowledge and their ignorance. Jesus knows, through charismatic insight, that Lazarus is dead and chooses to use the common metaphor of sleep to communicate the fact. The disciples, who do not have access as yet to such pneumatic inspiration, completely fail to grasp what Jesus is saying. They are portrayed yet again as the victims of misunderstanding (another common theme in John) whilst Jesus is portrayed as the recipient of divine *gnosis* (knowledge).

In terms of generic mode, we might put it this way: the disciples function as the buffoon figure in a story which has an essentially comic plot-shape. When Thomas (the only named individual in this group) speaks out in v.16, this comic ignorance finds its climactic expression. Thomas exclaims, 'Let us also go, that we may die with him'. Thomas, who also features in 14.5 and 20.24–29, is now seen as the epitome of the Johannine phenomenon of misunderstanding. As C.K. Barrett puts it:

> Thomas' remark looks back to v.8, apparently ignoring, or mistaking, the answer given by Jesus in vv.9f. His proposal, though it shows courage and devotion to the person of Jesus, shows also a complete failure to grasp the significance of Jesus'

death as it is presented in John; it is unthinkable that such a death should be shared.

(Barrett 1978: 394)

In phase 2 of the story (vv.17–37) two minor characters take the stage, Martha and Mary. They have been introduced by the narrator in vv.1–3 and in v.5. There we are informed that they are sisters, that they lived in Bethany, that they had a brother named Lazarus, that he had fallen seriously ill, that they had sent word of this to Jesus, and that they and their brother were loved by Jesus. It is further stated that Mary had poured perfume on the feet of Jesus, which she had then wiped with her hair (v.2). This, as I demonstrated earlier, is actually yet to happen in the story time of the gospel (12.1–3).

The role of the two sisters in John 11.1–44 is crucial to the plot. Martha appears first. She goes out alone to meet Jesus and, like the Samaritan woman in John 4, is portrayed as one who grows in faith and understanding. In v.21 she expresses her faith in Jesus as a charismatic healer by telling him that her brother would not have died had he been present (v.21). She then indicates a tentative faith in Jesus as someone more than just a healer by saying, 'I know that even now God will give you whatever you ask' (v.22). Behind these words there appears to be an implied faith in Jesus' ability to raise the dead. Jesus replies by saying, 'Your brother will rise again'. Martha's next remark shows that she regards this as a future event: 'I know he will rise again in the resurrection at the last day' (v.24), a common doctrinal tenet of Pharisaic Judaism. Jesus then leads her from a futuristic to a realized eschatology by saying, 'I am the resurrection and the life' (v.25). With this, traditional Jewish theology produces a true Christological confession. Martha exclaims, 'I believe that you are the Christ, the Son of God, who was to come into the world'. Martha here exhibits complete faith (20.31). She has moved from her two 'I know's' (v.22, v.24) to her climactic 'I believe' (27).

At v.28, Martha goes back and calls Mary. In performing these actions, her role develops from confessor to witness. Like the Samaritan woman in 4.28, she fetches someone else and encourages them to go to Jesus – in this case, Mary. Mary, Martha's sister, has been sitting at home. She gets up quickly and goes to the place where Martha had met Jesus. Jesus is still there. She falls at his feet and cries, repeating her sister's lament, 'Lord, if you had

been here, my brother would not have died'. Whilst Martha
expresses her grief by speaking of her brother's future resurrection,
Mary expresses hers by throwing herself at Jesus' feet in wild
despair. Indeed, the extreme pathos of her response is so intense
that Jesus himself is said to weep. So whilst Martha is used to elicit
an understanding of Jesus' divinity (the I-Am who raises the dead),
Mary is used to evoke an understanding of Jesus' humanity (the
Saviour who weeps with compassion). Both minor characters are
used by the author as foils.

The Jews who are introduced in v.33 have a similar function,
though they are not used in an identical way. They function as
a kind of dramatic chorus, commenting on the action involving
Jesus and the two sisters. As so often in John, they are a group
characterized by ambivalence. Some are clearly weeping (v.33) and
saying, 'See how he loved him' (v.36). Others are more cynical,
asking why he who opened the eyes of the man born blind (John
9) could not have prevented Lazarus from dying (v.37). This
division of opinion is carried over into the next episode (11.45ff)
when, after the miracle, some of these Jews put their faith in Jesus
(v.45) whilst others go to the Pharisees as informers (v.46). As
always in John, the *Ioudaioi* (Jews) are not to be trusted.

The only other minor character in the episode is of course
Lazarus himself. Lazarus is one of those named individuals, like
Nicodemus and Nathanael, who are distinctive to John's gospel.
He is the object of all the action in this story. He is introduced
in v.1 as an *asthenon*, a sick man (cf.v.3). It is to his tomb that
Jesus travels, risking his life. It is around his death that the
dialogue revolves. It is his restoration to life which is the climax
of the story. Within all this, Lazarus never says a word and only
performs one action, his emergence from the tomb. The only
development in his characterization is from being referred to as
a sick man in vv.1–3, to 'the dead man' (*ho tethnekos*) in v.44. His
is an entirely passive role, yet much is made of him. He is the one
character in the gospel thus far who is described in an intimate
relationship with Jesus. Lazarus is beloved of Jesus. The narrator
stresses this in v.5. The Jews stress it in v.36. Jesus himself stresses
it in his description of Lazarus as 'our friend' (v.11). Everywhere
the narrator seems to be taking trouble to depict Lazarus as a
particularly beloved disciple.

SOURCE

It is at this point that some comments concerning the source for the Lazarus episode are in order. We have looked in some detail at the narrative dynamics and the literary style of John 11.1–44. Now it is appropriate to consider what source the author was using when he composed this complex and multivalent narrative. This matter is of some importance. Though I will express my views tentatively, the composition theory which I shall propose here is one which will help to underline the narrative artistry and style of the author.

Broadly speaking, one of the following solutions is usually offered by scholars: (1) that John invented the whole story and that it is therefore a fiction; (2) that John composed this story from disparate materials in the Synoptic Gospels, and that it is therefore a fiction based on some traditional material; (3) that John wrote down the reminiscences of the beloved disciple who witnessed the whole episode, and that John 11.1–44 is therefore a faithful account of an historical event.

I find none of these three solutions satisfying. The first solution is usually expressed by those who have ruled out the possibility of such a miracle on a priori, philosophical grounds. They dismiss the Lazarus episode as a symbolic fiction on the basis that such a supernatural restoration to life could not happen now and would therefore not have happened then. But such an assertion (rarely supported by detailed argument) is not as cogent as it may at first appear. Contemporary experience of the Spirit within both the Pentecostal and the charismatic churches would suggest that such a demonstration of spiritual power as we see in John 11.1–44 is by no means implausible. Indeed, with the emergence of the Pentecostal movement this century, a large number of miraculous events have become more normative, including tongues, prophecy and healing. To those who do our biblical scholarship from within such churches, there is no problem in accepting the kind of story which we read about in John 11. It describes a supernatural event which is of the same genre as events we witness ourselves. The Lazarus episode need therefore not be relegated to the level of fiction.

The second solution fares little better. The view that the author created the Lazarus episode out of disparate data in the Synoptic Gospels raises more questions than it answers. For example, it is often argued that John has read the Lukan parable of Lazarus and the rich man (Luke 16.19–31), which ends with Jesus' comment, 'If they do not listen to Moses and the Prophets, they will not be convinced even if someone rises from the dead'. Some scholars argue that John knew this parable and simply created a story of a man called Lazarus who really did come back from the dead. They argue, in short, that John created his story from the details of Luke's parable. In reality, however, the influence is probably the other way round. As many scholars have argued, Luke's parable is probably influenced by an actual event in which a poor man called Lazarus was raised from death by Jesus. This is the only possible explanation of the presence of Lazarus' name at the beginning of the parable in Luke 16. No other parable contains a proper name, and the only plausible reason is because Jesus invented a transcendent, moralistic fiction using a historical character (Lazarus) and an historical event (his death and restoration to life). The events of John's story, in short, influenced the Lukan parable.

The third solution, however, is no more convincing. The view that John 11.1–44 is an eyewitness, historical account in every detail fails to do justice to the amount of Johannine theology and artistry which has clearly been added to the source. C.H. Dodd rightly showed that the normal method of the author prior to John 11 is to have a miracle story followed by a long interpretative passage of speech material. Discourses, in short, follow narratives (see, for example, John 6). But Dodd found a good deal of significance in the fact that this does not happen in the Lazarus episode. Rather, the kind of material which we find in discourses before John 11 (which are permeated with the distinctive ideas of Johannine theology) are now woven into the narrative of the raising of Lazarus itself. Narrative and discourse are inseparably combined in John 11.1–44 (Dodd 1963: 228). This means that John 11.1–44 is far more than a plain, unadorned description of actual events. It is more likely a poetic, theological redescription of a source which described a miracle in a vivid, detached and laconic manner. It is a narrative source into which the author has inserted the kind of interpretative elaboration normally reserved for the discourses of either the narrator or of Jesus.

My proposal is that John 11.1–44 is based on a source which has considerable historical value, but that the author has also recast that source in his own distinctive, narrative *style*. The following represents a list of the literary features which the author may well have added:

1 The flashback to Mary's anointing of Jesus in 11.2, which the author has added as a means of linking the Lazarus episode with Jesus' death and resurrection. Mary's anointing of Jesus is, after all, for burial.

2 The saying of Jesus in v.4 concerning God's glory and the glorification of the Son through the miracle. The noun 'glory' and the verb 'glorify' are clearly Johannine. They are popular themes in John's gospel and reflect the evangelist's not Jesus' theology.

3 The aside concerning Jesus' love for the family, which seems redundant and which has a Johannine ring (cf. the theme of love in John 1).

4 The discussion between Jesus and the disciples in vv.8–16 which is not strictly relevant to the story and contains a number of Johannine concepts (e.g. light and darkness). It also furthers the portrayal of Jesus as the elusive Christ and the disciples as a group characterized by misunderstanding.

5 The reference to the Jews from Jerusalem. The *Ioudaioi* in 11.8, 37 are the hostile Jews who are certainly Johannine.

6 The exchange between Martha and Jesus in vv.23–27, with the 'I am' saying and the confession of Martha. The Christology of these verses is really too exalted for it to have been part of the original conversation (though it is not out of the question).

7 The reference to Jesus being outside the village in v.30, which has been edited into the account for reasons of narrative focus.

8 Verse 33, with its insight into Jesus' emotions, and v.35 with the corresponding allusions to Jesus' tears. These may have been added to the source for Christological reasons, though it is not implausible that Jesus did express deep feeling in the orginal scene.

9 The divided views of the Jews in vv.36–37, a theme which features elsewhere in John's gospel (cf. 7.30–31; 7.40–44; 10.19–21).

10 The reference to Jesus' anger in v.38. Though, again, see my note of caution under point 8.

11 The saying about glorification in v.40 (for the reasons suggested above in point 2).

12 Verse 42, which has key Johannine themes such as 'sending' and 'believing'.

Not all of these features will have originated from the author's imagination. The *mashal* concerning 'light' and 'darkness' in 11.9–10 may well have been uttered by the historical Jesus. This in turn may have circulated in a collection of proverbial sayings in the Johannine community, and the author may simply have decided to use this saying in the Lazarus episode because it seemed relevant at this point. Similarly, the 'I am' saying in John 11.25–26 almost certainly came from a source other than the author's mind. It is probable that it represents a saying of the Risen Jesus; in other words, a saying uttered by a charismatic prophet in the Johannine community, regarded by the community as a word from the exalted Christ, and then inserted into the narrative of the Lazarus episode because of its propriety. Also, Martha's confession in John 11.27, though probably not part of the original source, may well have come from Martha herself, especially if her prominence in John 11–12 is an indication of her importance in the Johannine community. So whilst much of the style of the Lazarus episode can be regarded as the creative work of the author, not all of the inserted material derives from the author's imagination.

What, then, did the original source look like? Once we remove the twelve features identified above, we are left with the following, unembellished story:

> Now a man named Lazarus was sick. He was from Bethany, which was two miles from Jerusalem, and was the village of Mary and her sister Martha. So the sisters sent word to Jesus.
>
> When he heard this, Jesus said to his disciples, 'Our friend Lazarus has fallen asleep; but I am going to wake him up'.
>
> As he approached Bethany, Jesus found that Lazarus had been dead for four days.
>
> When Martha heard that Jesus was coming, she went out to meet him, but Mary stayed at home.
>
> 'Lord,' Martha said to Jesus, 'if you had been here, my brother would not have died. But I know that even now God will give you whatever you ask'.
>
> After she had said this, Martha went back and called her sister Mary. 'The Teacher is here', she said, 'and is asking for you'. When Mary heard this, she got up quickly and went to him.
>
> When Mary reached the place where Jesus was and saw him, she fell at his feet and said, 'Lord, if you had been here, my brother would not have died'.
>
> 'Where have you laid him?' he asked.

'Come and see, Lord', she replied.

Jesus came to the tomb. It was a cave with a stone laid across the entrance. 'Take away the stone', he said.

'But Lord', said Martha, 'by this time there is a bad odour, for he has been there for four days.'

But they took away the stone. Then Jesus looked up and said, 'Father, I thank you that you have heard me'.

With that, Jesus called out in a loud voice, 'Lazarus, come out!' The dead man came out, his hands and feet wrapped with strips of linen, and a cloth around his face.

Jesus said to them, 'Take off the grave clothes and let him go'.

TRADITION

There are a number of features about this hypothesized source which may well derive from good historical tradition. In what follows I will construct a list which will help to balance the twelve items identified above as the work of the author.

1 The introduction of the sick man as 'Lazarus of Bethany' is historical. 'The fixed combination "Lazarus of Bethany" characterizes him in a similar way to "Jesus of Nazareth" (1.45) or "Nathanael from Cana in Galilee" (21.2) as a historical figure' (Schnackenburg 1980: 321).

2 The topographical detail, 'Bethany was fifteen stadia from Jerusalem' is historically accurate. It is also geographically correct. We should note that John's source betrays a good knowledge of the topography of Jerusalem elsewhere (5.2; 9.2). So the note about where Bethany is situated is likely to be original.

3 The description of Lazarus as 'asleep' is likely to be historical. Jesus uses the same metaphor for Jairus' daughter in Mark 5.39b.

4 The portrayal of the two sisters, Mary and Martha. Luke also mentions these two sisters by name (Luke 10.38–42) and his view of them is remarkably similar to John's. John has Martha rushing out first and Mary sitting quietly at home. This comports well with Luke's portrayal of Martha as the pragmatic activist and Mary as the passive contemplative. Clearly John and Luke are both drawing on accurate historical tradition.

5 The presence of the two sisters at the scene. It is a feature of the

other two resurrection miracles in the Synoptics (Mark 5.40, Luke 7.12) that family members are present. The presence of the sorrowing siblings in the Lazarus episode is surely historical.

6 The identical words of Martha and Mary to Jesus ('Lord, if you had been here my brother would not have died') are plausible. The vocative 'Lord' (*kurie*) probably meant little more than 'Sir', so need not be removed. Furthermore, the identical sentiments of both sisters has a ring of truth. Anyone who does a good deal of pre-funeral visiting (as I do) will know how this sort of thing happens. Often family members sit around at home reminiscing and reflecting, so that, by the time the minister visits, certain sentiments are being shared and articulated by different family members in identical words. This is probably what happened in the case of Martha and Mary.

7 The details concerning the tomb may be historical. This is described as a *spelaios*, a 'cavern' with a stone laying upon the entrance (*epekeito epi*). 'What is displayed as the tomb of Lazarus today matches this description' (Schnackenburg 1980: 338).

8 Martha's concern for the smell of her brother's body may be an historical reminiscence. It is a very vivid and history-like detail.

9 The prayer of Jesus, which is merely a word of thanks, is possibly historical. 'Father' was Jesus' distinctive form of address for God in prayer, and thanksgiving was a frequent feature of his prayers. He uttered many *berakhot* (prayers of thanksgiving). The use of a *berakhah* at this point (in its original form, 'Blessed art thou O Lord for hearing me') is entirely plausible.

10 The details concerning the dead man's grave clothes strike one as historical. They are very precisely described as *keiriai* – 'strips of linen' – and a *soudarion* – 'head-cloth'.

11 The actual restoration of the dead man can be regarded as an historical event. If we are right in saying that an historical occurrence produced the mention of Lazarus in Luke's parable, then an event like this may well have happened to produce the mention of resurrection in the Lukan story.

12 The whole conduct of Jesus himself has an aura of plausibility here. We should note the number of similarities between the way he raises Lazarus and the way Mark says he raised Jairus' daughter. In both episodes, Jesus allows himself to be delayed and finds the sick person has already died on his arrival. In both stories Jesus uses the metaphor of sleep. In both stories

Jesus issues a command to bring the dead person back to life (see Mark 5.41), and in both stories Jesus gives a practical order after the raising ('feed her' in Mark 5.43b; 'Take off the grave clothes' in John 11.44). These very broad similarities suggest that John's source is descriptive of a particular *modus operandi* used by Jesus in the restoring of dead people to life.

In my opinion, these twelve features are the kinds of detail which one would expect from someone who had actually been present at the miracle itself. But then who was this eyewitness? At this point we should keep in mind that John's gospel derives from a rather unique source. Whilst Mark's gospel is supposed to be based on Peter's reminiscences (with Matthew and Luke following Mark, but also using other primitive sources including Q), John's gospel claims that its own historical tradition derives from an unnamed companion of Jesus known as 'the beloved disciple'. This anonymous disciple is mentioned in John 13.23–25, 18.15–16, 19.25–27, 20.3–9, 21.7, 21.20–24. On two occasions he is identified as the eyewitness responsible for memories preserved in the gospel (19.35; 21.24). Thus, the fourth gospel can be said to originate from the eyewitness testimony of an anonymous disciple. This tradition was independent from those which lie behind the Synoptic gospels, though it has similarities at a number of points.

The significance of this for the narrative source of the Lazarus episode should not be missed. The beloved disciple is, after all, portrayed as a Judean follower who usually appears in the environs of Jerusalem (see 13.23, 18.15, 20.3). Since the narrator makes a point of reminding us that Bethany is close to Jerusalem (11.18) we can make a case for the beloved disciple's presence at the events of John 11.1–44. This would incidentally explain why the raising of Lazarus is not to be found in Mark, Matthew and Luke. The Synoptic gospels focus mainly on the ministry of Jesus in Galilee. This is because their sources derive from the twelve Galilean apostles, specifically Peter. John's gospel, on the other hand, focuses mainly on the ministry of Jesus in Jerusalem. This is because its source derives from the unnamed Judean figure, called 'the beloved disciple'. The Lazarus episode is not included in the Synoptics most probably because of their concentration on the Galilean ministry of Jesus. A Bethany miracle, even a resurrection miracle, may have been regarded as redundant precisely because of its non-Galilean setting.

STYLE

What we have in the case of John 11.1–44 is therefore a narrative source which has been reworked by the author. In the process of redescribing the Lazarus episode, the distinctive characteristics of the author's style have been identified in the analysis above. As a summary, we might underline the following:

1 First of all, we should note the careful way in which the author 'contextualizes' this episode. It is not clumsily situated. Rather, it is the pivotal and crucial scene of the gospel. Jesus' restoration of Lazarus is seen as the act which secures Jesus' fate. In setting the Lazarus episode in this kind of context, the author even manages to achieve a clever effect of paradox: the giving of life to Lazarus is the act which leads to the taking of life from Jesus.

2 The author tells this story in such a way as to highlight its uniqueness. The Lazarus episode is made to stand as the seventh miracle in the gospel, and this highlights the author's creative use of number patterns (seven being a symbol of perfection). This uniqueness is given further emphasis by virtue of the formal distinctiveness of the story. It has few similarities with the other miracles in the gospel. Unlike them, in John 11.1–44 the miracle occurs at the end of the episode.

3 The author shows evidence of conscious and careful plotting of the narrative source. Events are organized into three clear phases (a beginning, a middle, and an end) which are underlined through the artful use of settings and focus (outside Judea, outside Bethany, outside the tomb). They are also organized temporally in such a way that a noticeable deceleration in the pace of the narrative occurs. The first part of the story takes a period of two or three days, whilst the rest of the story takes a period of a few minutes.

4 The author creates a kind of hologrammatic effect in the redescription of the story. The Lazarus episode is made a kind of microcosm of the whole gospel. Thus, the author's use of time in John 11.1–44 corresponds to the use of time in the gospel as a whole. The deep structure of the episode is made to resemble the deep structure of the whole gospel. The same is true for the generic mode of John 11.1–44 which, like the gospel in its entirety, presents the reader with an essentially comic U-shaped process.

5 The author uses prolepses or 'flash-forwards' as a means of reinforcing this microcosmic function of the Lazarus episode. The whole story of the gospel is constantly evoked in John 11.1–44 through echo effects with the death and resurrection of Jesus. This underlines the author's highly complex use of the narrator in this story. The narrator requires the reader to read the middle of the gospel (John 11.1–44) from the perspective of its ending (particularly John 20). This creates a kind of realized eschatology not only in the content of the gospel, but also in its form.

6 The author does much more with character than is evident in the source. Jesus' Messianic and even divine status is given great emphasis in his 'I am' saying, and in Martha's confession. The disciples are given more emphasis (with specific attention given to Thomas), as is Martha and the Jews. All of these minor characters are developed in order to evoke aspects of Jesus' character. In short, they are employed as foils.

7 Key themes are brought into the source, themes such as Jesus' elusiveness, the misunderstanding of the disciples, the division of the Jews, life, sending, believing and glorification. These are the author's *Leitworter* or keywords. They are features of his style.

In all these and other ways, the author redescribes the original story in his own distinctive style. In the process, the historical event of the raising of Lazarus is by no means destroyed or obscured. As John Robinson said of the gospel as a whole:

> One gets the strong impression that fact is sacred ... The theology is drawing out the history rather than creating it or even moulding it. It is an exercise in 'remembering', in the pregnant Johannine sense of reliving the events 'from the end', through the mind of the interpreter Spirit, presenting what they 'really' meant, in spirit and in truth. It is a meta-history; not any the less historical the more theologically it is understood, but the depth and truth of the history.
>
> (Robinson 1985: 297)

CONCLUSION

To sum up: this narrative-critical study of John 11.1–44 has been both synchronic and diachronic, literary and historical. We have studied the stylistic features of the author as evidenced in the final form of the story, and then thrown these into even sharper relief through a tentative examination of the way in which the author develops an original, narrative *Vorlage*. Our final comments will deal with an evaluation of John's style in the Lazarus episode.

In his 1923 essay on 'John's Narrative Style' which I quoted at the start of this chapter, Hans Windisch was severely critical of the 'unfinished' nature of the Lazarus story. He was appreciative of many aspects of its literary style (as we have been here) but harsh in his comments concerning its ending. Too much was left unsaid for his liking. John 11.1–44 is a fine symphony, to be sure, but it semed to Windisch far too like an unfinished symphony. As he put it:

> The dramatic shape of the conclusion leaves something to be desired from our point of view: there is no description of the immediate impression the resurrection makes, especially the greeting between brother and sisters, a corresponding gesture, or a word from Jesus along the lines of Luke 7.15's 'he gave him back to his mother', the touching conclusion to the family novella. The scene is broken off prematurely; the creative touch goes lame . . .
>
> (Windisch cited in Stibbe 1993b: 37)

If we are to pinpoint a weakness in the Lazarus episode, this would have to be it. To a degree, Windisch's complaint is partly due to expectations which are not appropriate. It is John's narrative style to leave a good deal unsaid. However, some of what Windisch says is justified. Whilst much of the narrative style of the Lazarus episode is exceedingly rich, as we have already seen, there are some weaknesses in the beginning and the ending of the piece. The beginning is too long, slowed up considerably by a somewhat redundant exchange between Jesus and the disciples. The ending is too short, with a lack of reaction except by the Judeans in 11.45–46. In short, the beginning is delayed and the ending is abrupt. So what Culpepper says of the gospel as a whole could certainly be said of the narrative style of John 11.1–44, that it is 'magnificent, but flawed' (1983: 231).

Chapter 5

'Polemic'

THE ETHICS OF RECEPTION

Sooner or later, all readers of John's gospel have to confront an apparent paradox. In the fourth gospel there are, on the one hand, clear statements about the love of God for the world. As early as John 3.16 we are told, 'God so loved the world that he gave his one and only Son, that whoever believes in him shall not perish but have eternal life'. In the unfolding narrative, this divine *agape* ('sacrificial love') is demonstrated in many of Jesus' words and actions, not least the raising of Lazarus which forms the centre-point in the plot of the gospel. There the Jews say of Jesus, 'See how much he loved him'.

On the other hand, the reader is also faced by the icy wind of a much sterner emotion in the gospel. This emotion surfaces in the many rebukes which we find on the lips of Jesus. Most unsettling of all are Jesus' diatribes against the Jews. How are we to react to the following?

> You are of your father, the devil, and your will is to do your father's desires. He was a murderer from the beginning, and has nothing to do with the truth, because there is no truth in him. When he lies, he speaks according to his own nature, for he is a liar and the father of lies. . . . The reason why you do not hear my words is because you are not of God.
>
> (John 8.44, 47)

Passages like these present an enormous problem to any contemporary reader of the fourth gospel. Here we are confronted with the paradox of 'a Gospel that proclaims love for the world while fostering hatred for Jews' (Culpepper, 1987: 285).

In recent times, we have become painfully aware of the persistence of Christian anti-Semitism throughout church history. Popular books such as *Faith and Fratricide, Shadows of Auschwitz, The Crucifixion of the Jews,* and *The Longest Hatred* (cited by Dan Cohn-Sherbok 1992: xi) all show how the seeds of anti-Semitism were sown in Christian sources like John's gospel and then nurtured throughout the history of the church. The most recent book arguing this case has been Dan Cohn-Sherbok's *The Crucified Jew: Twenty Centuries of Christian Anti-Semitism.* He argues that this anti-Semitism began with the New Testament itself. Although Cohn-Sherbok does admit that the origins of this Judeophobia also lie in the Graeco-Roman world prior to the New Testament, his argument is that the strongest roots of anti-Semitism lie in the tendency of writers like John to interpolate into their gospel accounts conflicts between Jesus and the leaders of the Jewish nation. Of the Scripture cited above (John 8.44, 47), Cohn-Sherbok writes:

> Not surprisingly, such a diatribe against the Jews and the Jewish faith has served as a basis for Christian persecution of the Jews through the centuries.

> (Cohn-Sherbrok 1992: 24)

So what are we to do with those passages in John which have fuelled such an Adversos Judaeos tradition in Christendom? Frances Young proposes that what is required is an ethical reading of such texts. She points to the recent movement in literary criticism known as 'the ethics of reception' (1993: 108). She quotes George Steiner's remark that 'no serious writer, composer, painter has ever doubted . . . that his work bears on good and evil' (cited by Young 1993: 109). If that is so, then we must approach texts ethically. That is to say, we must approach them with a desire to ask ethical questions, such as 'Did the author intend this text to be used as an instrument of social oppression?' In the case of passages like John 8.31–59, with its atmosphere of apparent anti-Semitism, this is particularly important. What are we to do with a text which appears to encourage such ardent prejudice?

Frances Young suggests that the only way of rescuing a text like John 8.31f is by resorting to allegorical interpretation:

> Might it not be expedient to allegorize 'the Jews' in John's Gospel so as to appropriate a text whose destructive effects have become embarrassing in the post-holocaust world?

> (Young 1993: 108)

I have some sympathy with this view, but there are problems with simply allegorizing the Jews in John. Allegorical readers are likely to pass over the intricacies and complexities of the relevant texts by quickly transforming Jewish groups into moral *exempla*. It is my argument in this chapter, however, that an ethical reading of Johannine polemic must develop out of a careful literary and historical study of the offending texts. In this chapter I will therefore take one text and expose it to a rigorous literary-historical analysis. The text I have chosen is John 8.31–59 because it is the text which is most often cited by Jewish authors as the *locus classicus* of New Testament anti-Semitism. It is my belief that a full appreciation of the literary dynamics of this text, and a proper understanding of its original historical function, may well shed some light on how we can read such passages in an ethical way.

The full NIV translation of the episode is as follows:

[31]To the Jews who had believed him, Jesus said, 'If you hold to my teaching, you are really my disciples. [32]Then you will know the truth, and the truth will set you free.'

[33]They answered him, 'We are Abraham's descendants and have never been slaves of anyone. How can you say that we shall be set free?'

[34]Jesus replied, 'I tell you the truth, everyone who sins is a slave to sin. [35]Now a slave has no permanent place in the family, but a son belongs to it for ever. [36]So if the Son sets you free, you will be free indeed. [37]I know you are Abraham's descendants. Yet you are ready to kill me, because you have no room for my word. [38]I am telling you what I have seen in the Father's presence, and you do what you have heard from your father.'

[39]'Abraham is our father', they answered. 'If you were Abraham's children', said Jesus, 'then you would do the things Abraham did. [40]As it is, you are determined to kill me, a man who has told you the truth that I heard from God. Abraham did not do such things. [41]You are doing the things your own father does.'

'We are not illegitimate children', they protested. 'The only Father we have is God himself.'

[42]Jesus said to them, 'If God were your Father, you would love me, for I came from God and now am here. I have not come on my own; but he sent me. [43]Why is my language not clear to you? Because you are unable to hear what I say. [44]You belong to your

father, the devil, and you want to carry out your father's desire. He was a murderer from the beginning, not holding to the truth, for there is no truth in him. When he lies, he speaks his native language, for he is a liar and the father of lies. [45]Yet because I tell you the truth, you do not believe me! [46]Can any of you prove me guilty of sin? If I am telling you the truth, why don't you believe me? [47]He who belongs to God hears what God says. The reason you do not hear is that you do not belong to God.'

[48]The Jews answered him, 'Aren't we right in saying that you are a Samaritan and demon-possessed?'

[49]'I am not possessed by a demon', said Jesus, 'but I honour my Father and you dishonour me. [50]I am not seeking glory for myself; but there is one who seeks it, and he is the judge. [51]I tell you the truth, if anyone keeps my word he will never see death.'

[52]At this the Jews exclaimed, 'Now we know that you are demon-possessed! Abraham died and so did the prophets, yet you say that if anyone keeps your word, he will never taste death.

[53]Are you greater than our father Abraham? He died, and so did the prophets. Who do you think you are?'

[54]Jesus replied, 'If I glorify myself, my glory means nothing. My Father, whom you claim as your God, is the one who glorifies me. [55] Though you do not know him, I know him. If I said I did not, I would be a liar like you, but I do know him and keep his word. [56]Your father Abraham rejoiced at the thought of seeing my day; he saw it and was glad.'

[57]'You are not yet fifty years old', the Jews said to him, 'and you have seen Abraham!'

[58]'I tell you the truth', Jesus answered, 'before Abraham was born, I am!' [59]At this, they picked up stones to stone him, but Jesus hid himself, slipping away from the temple grounds.

CONTEXT

As we saw in Chapter 4, responsible interpretation begins with the elucidation of the context of a literary text. First we must appreciate its *overall* context.

John 8.31–59 occurs in the second major section of the gospel: John 5.1–10.42. In this section, conflict appears in the plot of the narrative. In the first major section (John 2–4), there are only occasional hints of conflict between Jesus and the Jews or the

Pharisees. In John 2.13–25, Jesus enters into dialogue with the Jews in Jerusalem after the cleansing of the temple. Surprisingly, however, there is no note of hostility from the Jews at this point. In John 3.1–21, Jesus enters into dialogue with Nicodemus, a Pharisee and member of the ruling Jewish council. But here there is no sense of conflict either. To be sure, Nicodemus – like the Jews in John 2.19–21 – misunderstands Jesus, but there is no heated exchange of words apart from Jesus', 'You are Israel's teacher and you do not understand these things?' (3.10). In John 4, the only suggestion of conflict is in the itinerary fragment inserted at John 4.1–3, where the narrator informs us that the Pharisees had heard about Jesus' ministry of baptism, and that Jesus therefore left Judea. Even here, however, there is no narratorial aside explaining that this evasive action was due to hostility.

If conflict is absent from the plot in John 2–4, it is overtly present in John 5–10. Indeed, there is a very abrupt *desis* or 'complication' at the start of Chapter 5. After Jesus has healed the man at the pool of Bethesda, a controversy arises between Jesus and the Jews. Jesus has performed this miracle on the sabbath, so the Jews start to persecute him (5.16). Jesus explains that his Father in heaven works on the sabbath. At this point the Jews are said to try 'all the harder to kill him' (5.18), implying that there had already been attempts to put Jesus to death which the narrator omits. So now the note of conflict increases dramatically. In John 6, Jesus' preaching is met with grumbling from the Jews (6.41) and with desertion by a group of disciples, who find it *skleros . . . logos*, hard teaching (6.60, 66). In John 7, the hostility of the Jews is intensified. At the start of John 7, the Jews are portrayed watching out for Jesus (7.11). In 7.14 Jesus starts teaching in the temple courts. Some accuse him of being 'demon-possessed' (7.20), others try to seize him (7.30), the temple guards are finally sent to arrest him (7.32), but fail to bring him in.

At this point we arrive at chapter 8, and here we must move to a discussion of the *immediate* context of John 8.31–59. John 8.31–59 is the final in a series of seven controversy-dialogues extending from 7.1 to 8.59. C.H. Dodd describes John 7–8 as the 'central block of the Book of Signs' (1965: 346–6). The seven controversy-dialogues which make up this block of material follow an introductory section in 7.1–10 and a brief scene in 7.11–13:

7.14–24	First dialogue:	Moses and Christ
7.25–36	Second dialogue:	the claims of Jesus
7.37–44	Third dialogue:	the claims of Jesus
7.45–52	Fourth dialogue:	the claims of Jesus
8.12–20	Fifth dialogue:	the claims of Jesus
8.21–30	Sixth dialogue:	the claims of Jesus
8.31–59	Seventh dialogue:	Abraham and Christ

Though the links between each dialogue are not obvious, Dodd maintains that the material as a whole is united by four literary features; first, by the conflict between Jesus and the ecclesiastical leaders of Judaism, a consistent feature throughout John 7–8; secondly, by the tone, which is 'markedly polemical' at all times; thirdly, by the setting in the temple courts during the feast of Tabernacles; fourthly, by the *inclusio* between the beginning of John 7 and the closure at John 8.59 (1965: 346–8). Of this fourth feature, Dodd points out that John 7 begins with Jesus travelling *en krupto*, 'in secret' (7.4) and ends with him hiding himself (*ekrube*, 8.59). As Dodd writes:

> The words *en krupto-ekrube* may be taken as clamping this entire series of dialogues into a dramatic unity, with the Feast of Tabernacles to provide a significant background to the whole.
>
> (Dodd 1965: 348)

From these observations we can conclude the following about context: the *overall* context of the passage is the second section of John 1–12 (often called the Book of Signs). This second section extends from John 5–10 and is characterized by growing conflict between Jesus and the Jewish hierarchy in Jerusalem. The *immediate* context of John 8.31–59 is a series of seven dialogues stretching from the beginning of John 7 to the end of John 8. John 8.31–59 is the final dialogue in this series. This episode is clearly marked off from the rest. There is a sense of closure at the end of John 8.30: 'Even as he spoke, many put their faith in him'. A new episode then begins with the narrator's introduction of a different audience, 'the Jews who had believed him' (perfect participle). We shall examine the identity and the nature of this specific grouping in the section on 'characterization' below.

GENRE

The second step towards a responsible interpretation of John 8.31–59 is the discovery of its genre. Richard Burridge has recently argued that:

> Genre is a system of communication of *meaning*. Before we can understand the meaning of a text, we must master its genre. Genre will then be our guide to help us re-construct the original meaning, to check our interpretation to see if it is valid, and to assist in evaluating the worth of the text and communication.
>
> (Burridge 1992: 52)

Since the discernment of the genre of John 8.31–59 is so important in the hermeneutical process, we must spend some time identifying the group of texts in ancient literature with which our passage shares the closest family resemblances.

In order to do this, we need to remind ourselves of Northrop Frye's helpful analysis of the four genres of literature: romance, tragedy, satire/irony and comedy (1971: 163–242) (see Chapter 3). These four *mythoi* or archetypal modes all have their own distinctive shape. Comedy has a U-shaped plot, which descends into bondage but then ascends to freedom. Tragedy has the opposite shape, with the hero ascending to a place of high honour but then descending into a terrible *pathos* (death-scene) suggestive of sacrifice. Romance has a plot which portrays a hero's quest in an idealized world of fairies, knights and beautiful maidens. Satire, on the other hand, presents a world which is the very opposite of ideal – a realistic narrative world in which the sins of humanity are cruelly, sometimes humorously exposed.

As we saw in Chapter 3, Hayden White has taken Frye's categories and applied them to history-writing (1978). White claims that an historian shapes a series of events into a narrative because life does not have the shape of a story; it does not possess narrativity. Stories are told but they are not lived. Consequently, when an historian seeks to create a reconstruction of past events, s/he has to emplot events in a coherent and meaningful sequence. In the process, s/he will employ a particular point of view, and that point of view is expressed using one of Frye's four archetypal genres of romance, tragedy, satire/irony or comedy. That is why Michelet describes the French revolution in a style clearly marked by 'romance', whilst Tocqueville reconstructs the same history in a style which is overtly 'tragic'. Every historian matches a set of events with a particular plot-structure. This process of matching events with plots is not an easy task because there is nothing intrinsically romantic, tragic, satirical or comic about history. The decision to use a certain *mythos* or generic mode depends on the perspective of the historian.

What is true of historians in general is also true of the author of the fourth gospel, who was writing narrative historiography. John also 'emplotted' his story according to certain generic conventions. So which generic mode did he choose in the case of John 8.31–59? When we examine this text closely it quickly becomes obvious that he did not choose 'romance'. There is nothing idealized or dream-like about this confrontation between Jesus and the Jews. Nor did John choose a tragic perspective. Though Jesus is the target of abusive comments, he is in fact much more the one who victimizes than the one who is victimized. Nor did John choose a comic perspective to redescribe this conflict between Jesus and his opponents. There is no hope of forgiveness or of reconciliation in this clash of personalities. The conflict is left unresolved both here and in the rest of the gospel. This only leaves satire. Is John 8.31–59 satirical history? Is Jesus' seventh and climactic dialogue in John 7–8 an example of what George Test calls 'aesthetic aggression, an artful attack, a creative assault'? (1991: 4).

In order to answer this we must define 'satire' a little more closely. The word 'satire', however, is notoriously elusive. One writer has likened defining satire to 'trying to put a shadow in a sack' (Test 1991: 13). Etymology does not help much. Cocker's *English Dictionary* (1704) defined the word as 'Anything sharp or severe', a definition based on the ancient word '*satyrus*', 'an hairy monster, like a horned man with goat's feet'. Later on, however, a different root was proposed, '*satura*' – a kind of dish, a hotchpotch of many different ingredients. In the Augustan period in particular, satire was seen as 'a tasty dish to serve all palates, a sophisticated confection of sweet and sour' (Noakes 1987: 50).

Satire is clearly a flexible phenomenon, sometimes sharp (*satyrus*), sometimes more palatable (*satura*). Perhaps this is why John Dryden made his celebrated distinction between two different kinds of satire. The first kind Dryden described as 'raillery' or 'smiling satire'. This is exemplified by the Roman poet Horace, who always meant to make his readers laugh through the sophisticated use of wit. The second kind Dryden described as 'rallery' or 'snarling satire'. This is exemplified by the Roman poet Juvenal, who sought to evoke a sense of moral outrage through the use of 'saeva indignatio', savage indignation. This distinction subsequently became very popular. Joseph Trap wrote, 'Satire in *general,* is a poem design'd to reprove the Vices and Follies of Mankind: It is twofold: either the *jocose,* as that of *Horace*; or the *serious,* like that of *Juvenal* . . . The one is pleasant and facetious: the other angry and austere: the one smiles; the other storms' (Noakes 1987: 51).

The distinction between Horatian and Juvenalian satire is one which is primarily made on the basis of 'tone'. In Horatian satire, the tone is 'gentle, urbane, and smiling' (Ryken 1974: 262). Horatian satire 'aims to correct folly or vice by gentle and sympathetic laughter' (Ryken 1974: 262). Juvenalian satire, on the other hand, is 'biting, bitter, and angry. It points with contempt and moral indignation at the corruptness and evil of men and of institutions' (Ryken 1974: 262).

A secondary means of distinguishing these two kinds of satire is through structure. Horatian satire tends to be sophisticated and polished literature. 'The style is accomplished and the work of a craftsman' (Ryken 1974: 262). Juvenalian satire, on the other hand, tends to be less polished. As Ryken puts it:

> The writer of informal satire is much less of a literary craftsman, being preoccupied with content. He is much less likely to tell a well-designed story, for example, than to employ direct rebuke and invective. His form is often loose in structure, his style is direct and simple, and his work may approach something unliterary.
>
> (Ryken 1974: 262)

It is my conviction that an analysis of the tone and structure of John 8.31–59, as well as certain other literary features in the text, will confirm the satirical character of this final dialogue in John 7–8. Indeed, it will reveal that the genre of this text is best defined as informal satire – satire of the snarling rather than the smiling kind.

TONE

If John 8.31–59 is an example of informal satire, then the tone of the satirist will be biting, harsh, severe. This is exactly what we find. The words of Jesus in John 8.31f become more and more aggressive as the dialogue progresses from its apparently innocuous beginnings. This progression into full-blown satire needs to be noted carefully.

There is nothing overtly condemnatory in the opening words of Jesus:

> If you hold to my teaching, you are really my disciples. Then you will know the truth and the truth will set you free.
>
> (John 8.31–32)

However, his addressees – the Jews who had believed him (8.31) – react by saying they do not need to be liberated; they are children of Abraham, and therefore sons rather than slaves. Jesus then introduces the note of sin (8.34), a key theme in the drama. Sin, in John's gospel, is the failure to recognize and to believe in Jesus. This is precisely the problem here. Jesus' addressees are sinners, they do not believe in Jesus. Therefore Jesus utters an enigmatic *mashal* in which he portrays his audience as slaves (because they are in bondage to sin) rather than sons:

> Now a slave has no permanent place in the family, but a son belongs to it forever.
>
> (John 8.35)

At this point, the tone begins to change from one of mild criticism to one of indignation. The theme of 'murder', another key *topos*, enters the debate. Jesus says:

> I know you are Abraham's descendants. Yet you are ready to kill me, because you have no room for my word.
>
> (John 8.37)

The desire of these antagonists to murder Jesus reveals that Abraham cannot be their father ('father' is another of the *Leitworter* in this dialogue). If these Jews were really children of Abraham, then they would behave like Abraham. But the murderous intention of the Jews is proof of a very different paternity. The identity of this father-figure is held off until the next stage of the dialogue, which extends from 8.42–47.

In this unit of the text, dialogue gives way to monologue. Jesus is the only one who speaks in 8.42–47. Furthermore, harsh criticism here progresses to snarling invective. It is in these verses that one of the most passionate critiques of any Jewish group is to be found in the entire New Testament. Here Jesus refutes the claim that God is their father. Neither Abraham nor God can be said to be their father. Instead, their conduct provides the key to their paternity. Here Jesus expresses 'rallery' through *amplificatio* (the accumulation of topics):

You are unable to hear what I say (8.43).

You belong to your father, the devil, and you want to carry out your father's desire (8.44).

You do not believe me! (8.45).

The reason you do not hear is that you do not belong to God (8.47).

In these words, Jesus paints his antagonists in the worst possible colours. They are spiritually deaf, they are liars, they are guilty of unbelief, they are murderers. All this, says Jesus, points to the truth that the devil is their father.

In the final unit of the episode (8.48–59), the form returns to dialogue and the Jews react to Jesus' harsh invective. The Jews now indulge in name-calling, which shows that Jesus' words (like satire in general) have succeeded in generating more of the emotion he himself has vented. So the Jews accuse Jesus of being a Samaritan and of being demon-possessed (8.48). Jesus repudiates this charge by pointing to the way in which his conduct reveals the identity of his Father (8.49). Jesus then claims that those who keep his word will never taste death (8.51). This truly aggravates the Jews. Even Abraham died. How therefore can Jesus have the power to transcend death? Is he one greater than Abraham? Who does he think he is? (8.53). Jesus replies that he is not interested in personal honour. If there is any glory for Jesus, it is given by the Father. That glory and honour is profound indeed, for even Abraham rejoiced at the thought of seeing the coming of Jesus (8.56). The Jews reply with sarcasm, 'You're not fifty years old and you've seen Abraham!' Jesus concludes with a highly provocative word of revelation in which he uses the divine name ('I am') in its absolute form: 'Before Abraham was born, I am!' With this *lusis* or denouement, the Jews try to stone Jesus.

From this overview it is clear that John 8.31–59 qualifies as informal satire on the basis of 'tone'. The tone of Jesus is snarling not smiling, serious not jocose, angry not facetious. In particular, we should note how the author uses irony, invective and parody to strengthen his *saeva indignatio*.

The most obvious example of irony in the episode is the way in which the Jews deny the charge that they are murderers and then attempt to stone Jesus at the conclusion of the story. In this action, the ideal reader quickly perceives what the Jews fail to see: that their aggressive behaviour proves the very thing which they have so strenuously refuted, that they are 'murderers'. In this instance, therefore, John's irony serves his satire, as it does throughout the fourth gospel. Given this truth, it seems remarkable to me that none of the many studies of John's irony ever mention satire. If John's irony is subservient to his satire, then we would expect some discussion; but in reality this chapter is the first to examine the presence and use of 'satire' in the fourth gospel.

Another tone commonly used by satirists and visible in John 8.31–59 is 'invective'. Test defines invective as 'a general term indicating direct verbal attack on a person or thing through the use of vituperative language or ridicule' (1991: 103). Invective 'occurs when the aggressive element is uppermost, judgement is prominent, the play and laughter elements are minimal' (Test 1991: 33). It goes without saying that there is plenty of invective in the tone of Jesus' words in John 8.31–59. A full range of aggressive criticisms is hurled at the Jews in this story. From Jesus' lips we are told that they are lying, murderous, and spiritually blind. This is undoubtedly an example of the satirical use of invective.

Finally, the reader should note the tone of parody in Jesus' words. Jesus accuses the Jews in John 8.31–59 of being children of the devil, of hearing what their diabolical father is saying (8.38), and putting his murderous plan into action. In these words – as we saw in Chapter 2 – Jesus creates a parody of his own relationship with his heavenly Father. He too has a Father, he too hears what the Father is saying, he too does what his Father wants. Whilst the Jews in John 8.31–59 are busy trying to put Jesus to death (their father's plan), he is busy trying to bring life into the world (John 10.10; his Father's plan). In his critique of the Jews who had believed him, Jesus creates a grim parody of his own relationship with the Father. Like Jesus, these particular Jews do what their father is doing and hear what their father is saying.

STRUCTURE

If the variegated tones of the episode suggest the genre of informal satire, so does its structure. The structure of John 8.31–59 is loose. When one compares John 8.31–59 with the episode which immediately follows (the healing of the man born blind in John 9.1–41), this becomes very obvious. As a number of literary critics of the fourth gospel have noticed, John 9.1–41 is divided with consummate artistry into seven balancing scenes, all arranged into a neat, chiastic form:

A^1 1–7   The dialogue between Jesus and the disciples

B^1 8–12   The dialogue between the blind man and his neighbours

C^1 13–17   The dialogue between the Pharisees and the blind man

D   18–23   The dialogue between the Jews and the man's parents

C^2 24–34   The dialogue between the Pharisees and the blind man

B^2 35–38   The dialogue between Jesus and the blind man

A^1 39–41   The dialogue between Jesus and the Pharisees
(Duke 1985: 118)

When we compare this structure with what we find in John 8.31–59, the difference could not be more marked. In John 8.31–59, there is little sense of literary structure.

There is a basic structure to John 8.31–59 insofar as the episode is divided into three units:

A^1 31–41 The dialogue between Jesus and the Jews

B   42–47 The monologue of Jesus

A^2 48–59 The dialogue between Jesus and the Jews

There is also a sense of parallelism caused by the mention of Abraham in A^1 and A^2. In A^1 Abraham is mentioned in vv.37, 39, 40. In A^2, his name occurs in vv.52, 53, 56, 57. It does not occur at all in the middle unit (B).

But this, I propose, is as far as the sense of structure goes in John 8.31–59. Jerome Neyrey has recently argued to the contrary, saying that a further sense of structure is suggested by the repeated pattern of statement/misunderstanding/explanation which he finds in 8.31–59 (1988: 43). In this pattern, Jesus makes a statement, the Jews misunderstand it, then Jesus explains himself:

Statement	31–32	38	41a	51	56
Misunderstanding	33	39a	41b	52–53	57
Explanation	34–37	39b–40	42–47	54–55	58

However, this structure is by no means as obvious as Neyrey makes out. It omits vv.48–50 entirely (because here the Jews initiate the pattern, and Neyrey cannot have Jesus misunderstanding them!). Also, it depends upon separating parts of Jesus' statements which are, in the flow of the debate, connected logically. For example, 'You are doing the things your father does' (v.41) is separated from 'Abraham did not do such things' (v.40). So the structural use of *Missverstandnis* is not as evident in the whole of this episode as Neyrey argues.

What we therefore find is a text with far less structure than, say, John 9.1–41. All this is consistent with informal satire. Indeed, it is consistent with human nature, for which of us expresses our anger in well-ordered, iambic pentameters? The spontaneity and intensity of Jesus' indignation, in my opinion, speaks of his humanity. It is, like our own outbursts, more a matter of frenzy than of form.

SETTING

From this literary-critical analysis, it should be evident that John has chosen the genre of informal satire in the redescription of this heated exchange between Jesus and the Jews in 8.31–59. Two further observations will confirm the use of the satiric genre: first of all John's use of narrative setting, second the way in which he characterizes protagonist and antagonists.

As regards setting, the whole episode takes place in the capital city of Jerusalem. More specifically, it takes place during the crowded festival of Tabernacles which is mentioned at 7.2, 14, 37. At this feast, Jesus enters the temple courts (7.14; 8.59) and starts teaching. A great array of audiences are said to pass his way, to listen to his words, and to respond to what he says. In fact, there is a greater profusion of social groups in John 7–8 than anywhere else in the gospel. The following all appear in these chapters: the brothers of Jesus, the Jews, the crowds, the people of Jerusalem, the Pharisees, the temple guards, the chief priests, the Jews who had believed in him. Furthermore, amongst the crowds, there is profound confusion. Some of the crowd side with Jesus, some do not. They are divided:

Among the crowds there was widespread whispering about him. Some said, 'He is a good man.' Others replied, 'No, he deceives the people.' (7.12).

At this they tried to seize him, but no-one laid a hand on him, because his time had not yet come. Still, many in the crowd put their faith in him (7.30–31).

On hearing his words, some of the people said, 'Surely this man is the Prophet.' Others said, 'He is the Christ.' Still others asked, 'How can the Christ come from Galilee?' (7.40–41).

John's use of setting comports well with the genre of informal satire, for 'the scene of satire is always disorderly and crowded, packed to the very point of bursting' (Kernan 1959: 7). Most major works of satire depict a scene of 'disorderly profusion' (Kernan 1959: 8): the streets of Juvenal's Rome, Hogarth's 'Gin Lane', *Bartholomew Fair*, the City as the Dunces set off for Westminster, Don Juan's London streets that 'boil over with their scum', Nathanael West's Hollywood, Aldous Huxley's futuristic London. 'It is no accident that most satire is set in the city, particularly in the metropolis with a polyglot people' (Kernan 1959: 8). What Alvin Kernan says of the scene of satire in general applies very well to John's portrayal of the bustling, disordered city of Jerusalem in John 7–8. He writes:

> Every author of satire is free to stress the elements of the scene which appear most important to him, but beneath the divergencies of the surface the satiric scene remains fundamentally the same picture of a dense and grotesque world of decaying matter moving without form.
>
> (Kernan 1959: 12)

CHARACTERIZATION

If the tone, structure and setting of John 8.31–59 is consistent with the genre of informal satire, so is the characterization of protagonist and antagonists in this episode. If we examine the protagonist first, it is clear that the major feature of his characterization is forensic in character. Here Jesus is portrayed as a judge. 'Jesus conducts a trial in which some people are formally charged, tried, convicted, and sentenced' (Neyrey 1988: 37).

In this lawsuit scenario, John includes all the elements of a forensic process: 'a judge, a norm of judgment, testimony from witnesses, a judge's *cognitio,* formal charges, and proof' (Neyrey 1988: 48–9). The norm of judgment is God's. He stands behind the scene as the ultimate judge (8.50). Jesus only judges as the Father judges. The primary witness is Abraham. Jesus appeals to him in 8.56. A number of formal charges are made:

> You have no room for my word (8.37).
>
> You are doing the things your own father does (8.41).
>
> You are unable to hear what I say (8.43).
>
> You belong to the devil (8.44).
>
> You do not believe me (8.45).
>
> You do not belong to God (8.47).

The primary charge is that the Jews are, like the devil, *murderers.* Murder is one of the frequent subjects of legal trials. This trial in John 8.31–59 is no exception. The proof of this charge is the attempt on Jesus' life made in 8.59.

John's portrayal of Jesus as judge is influenced by the trial scenes in Isaiah 40–55, where Yahweh is also portrayed as judge. In each of these trial scenes, Yahweh summons the pagan nations to a place of judgment and asks them to provide witnesses concerning the reality of their gods. No testimony is brought forward, so Yahweh passes sentence: 'I am he'. The LXX (Septuagint) of 'I am' in Deutero Isaiah is *ego eimi*, which is the same phrase as used by Jesus, most notably in John 8 in the absolute form:

8.24: 'I told you that you would die in your sins if you do not believe that I am' (*ego eimi*)

8.28: 'When you have lifted up the Son of Man, then you will know that I am' (*ego eimi*)

8.58: 'Before Abraham was born, I am' (*ego eimi*).

The sense of intertextual resonances between John 8.31–59 and the trial scenes in Deutero Isaiah suggest the following implicit commentary: that Jesus is the equivalent of Yahweh the judge, the trial is the equivalent of the lawsuit in Deutero Isaiah, and the Jews are the equivalent of Isaiah's unbelieving pagans.

Such a use of the Isaianic *Gerichtsszene* cleverly serves John's satiric intention. John Oldham claimed that the satirist is 'Both Witness,

Judge, and Executioner' (cited in Test 1991: 30), George Test that 'Satire ultimately judges' (1991: 5), and Thomas Jemielity that satire is 'a form of justice' (1992: 40). If this is the case, then John's use of the Isaianic trial scene is intended for satiric effect. By using the forensic motifs of Isaiah's trial scenes, John is able to satirize the Jews who had believed Jesus in John 8.31–59.

This brings us to the antagonists in the controversy-dialogue. Who are they? We may begin by noting that they are a group of Jews who are portrayed as caricatures rather than as fully developed characters. Their function is simply to act as the satirical victim. David Morris defines this role as follows:

> The satirical victim has quasi-legal status as a malefactor; his arraignment is a form of poetic justice; and the satirist, after serving first as judge and jury, steps forward to carry out the necessary punishment, all for the public good. The reader, like the crowd at eighteenth century executions, holds the uneasy and sometimes alarming role of witness, for whom the spectacle of someone else's punishment cannot be entirely undisturbing.
>
> (Morris, cited in Jemielity 1992: 41–2)

In terms of satire, the antagonists in John 8.31–59 are the malefactors, Morris' 'satirical victim'.

If the antagonists are portrayed so darkly, we must be very careful to identify who they really are. John 8.31 introduces them as 'the Jews who had believed him'. The NIV translates *pepisteukotas* as a pluperfect (had believed) even though it is a perfect participle. This is partly justified by the context. The subsequent verses depict these believing Jews as a group who very quickly contradict Jesus, and even want to stone him by the end of the conversation (8.59). Only a group who '*had* believed' but were now about to fall away would behave like this. As Schnackenburg writes:

> The evangelist's real concern becomes apparent in v.31. He is addressing Jews who have been in the faith for some time [perfect participle]; the saying of Jesus that they must remain in his word applies to them.
>
> (Schnackenburg 1980: 204)

Schnackenburg's exegesis alerts us to the important truth that the Jews mentioned in 8.31 are Jewish disciples of Jesus who are about to apostatize in the ensuing narrative. This means that the Jews whom Jesus is satirizing in John 8.31–59 are not Jews in general;

they are Jewish believers who turn out, in the unfolding story, to have no room for Jesus' *logos* (8.37), to be incapable of holding on to the truth (8.44), unable to keep his word (8.51) and ultimately Christ-killers (8.59). This is a group of Jews who were followers of Jesus, but who then, under a pressure which is not described by the narrator, start to revert to their former religious beliefs. Instead of holding on to the teaching of Jesus, they now claim that Abrahamic descent is sufficient for membership of the covenant community and, by implication, for salvation. This being so, we must be very careful when we talk about *who* and *what* is being condemned in this episode. *Jesus is not attacking the Jewish people in general. Far from it. He is satirizing apostasy in 8.31–59. He is satirizing those who start on the road of discipleship, but who give up when the going gets tough.*

This point cannot be stressed more forcibly. John 8.31–59 is *not* anti-Semitic in the strict sense: i.e. against the Jewish people as a whole. Jesus is himself, in any case, a Jew. What Jesus is condemning is a particular group of Jews who exemplify a particular kind of unbelief. There are, broadly speaking, four types of relationship to Jesus enjoyed by Jews in John's gospel. There are first of all Jewish believers (the disciples); there are Jews who believe in secret (the crypto-believers of John 12.42); there are unbelieving Jews (for example, the Jews in John 10.22–39); there are finally the lapsed Jewish believers (mentioned in John 8.31f). If one were to draw a spectrum of faith responses from John's gospel, then Jewish believers (the disciples) would be at the positive end; the lapsed Jewish believers would be at the negative end. The lapsed Jews would, in other words, be in an even more reprehensible position than unbelieving Jews. They had believed Jesus (*pisteuein* plus dative, which must connote faith commitment), but in the unfolding drama of John 8.31f they fall away and turn against Jesus.

That John regards lapsed Jewish disciples as the worst of all sinners becomes particular evident when we examine the use of dualism in John 8.31–59. The whole episode explores various themes which are set up as 'binary oppositions' – oppositions which are never resolved:

Truth/error
Freedom/slavery
Divine/demonic
Hearing/not hearing
Obeying/not obeying

Life/death
Honour/shame
Knowledge/ignorance.

The judgment reserved for the apostate Jews is particularly damn-
ing. They are characterized in terms of the negative poles of each
binarism. They are sentenced to error, slavery, demonization,
deafness, disobedience, death, shame and ignorance. No one is
judged as fiercely or as negatively as this throughout the whole
course of John's story. This group is condemned 'with the most
devastingly dualistic epithets' (Meeks 1972: 49). Lapsed Jewish
believers are the lowest of the low, not because they are Jewish, but
because they are apostates.

Perhaps we can now see the importance of a rigorous literary
analysis of those texts in John which appear so offensively anti-
Semitic. John 8.31–59 is certainly the most horrific of all of these,
and yet we have seen the danger of jumping to conclusions too
quickly. Too often people assume that the satire of Jesus in John
8.31–59 is a satire of the Jewish people as a whole. Even Dan Cohn-
Sherbok is guilty of this in the quotation cited earlier. He writes of
John 8.31–59:

> Not surprisingly, *such a diatribe against the Jews and the Jewish faith*
> has served as a basis for Christian persecution of the Jews through
> the centuries [my emphasis].
>
> (Cohn-Sherbok 1992: 24)

But Jesus is not satirizing 'the Jews and Jewish faith', he is satirizing
Jews who had believed Jesus! Admittedly, the narrator does describe
the antagonists as *hoi Ioudaioi* in 8.48, 52 and 57. But this is
shorthand for the broader designation offered in 8.31, 'the Jews
who had believed him'. With reluctance one therefore has to admit
that Cohn-Sherbok (like countless Christian readers) has not read
the text carefully enough. John 8.31–59 is a satire of apostasy not
of Judaism. Indeed, the nationality and the race of the satirical
victim is, in one sense, irrelevant. The main thing is not that the
group is Jewish but that it has apostatized.

FUNCTION

We are now getting very close to the point where an ethical reading
of John 8.31–59 is a real possibility. However, one more question

needs to be answered. 'What social function did the author have in mind when he composed this satire of the apostate Jews? What was the original purpose of this satire in the context of the Johannine community?' Answering this question is extremely important if we are to interpret our passage responsibly. As Test rightly remarks, 'While some art may aim for self-sufficiency, satire remains bound to its communal origins and social function' (1991: 32). It always 'exists in a direct critical relationship with the society which produces it' (Noakes 1987: 2).

In order to answer the question, we need to remind ourselves briefly of the circumstances of the gospel's eventual publication. It is now something of a consensus amongst Johannine scholars that the fourth gospel was completed after a heated controversy between church and synagogue late in the first century CE. In about 85 CE, the twelfth benediction was reformulated by Rabbi Gamaliel II in Jamnia so as to include a curse against the Christian heretics – that is, Jewish Christians who were still worshipping in the synagogues with non-Christian Jews. It was then subsequently read out in the synagogues – along with the rest of the eighteen benedictions – in the last years of the first century. From this moment, it became impossible for Christians in the diaspora to remain within the fold of Judaism. Those who were identified as Christians were excommunicated from the synagogues by the local ruling Pharisees. John's gospel, it is argued, reflects this milieu and was written mainly to encourage Jewish Christians to keep believing in Jesus after the traumatic, social bereavement which they had faced.

These comments help us to reconstruct the historical background to John 8.31–59. The ultimate background lies in an incident involving the historical Jesus. The source behind John 8.31–59 was probably a controversy story which described an actual debate between Jesus and some of his Jewish contemporaries. The form of this source may have resembled the controversy stories of the synoptic gospels. As Hans Windisch proposed in 1923:

> The synoptics have numerous pericopae which are preserved in this stylistic form, and M. Albertz in particular has provided an excellent style-critical analysis of these synoptic controversy dialogues.

> (Windisch, cited in Stibbe 1993b: 49)

We may therefore conjecture that John 8.31–59 is based on source material which has recognizable parallels in the Synoptic tradition.

When we ask what group Jesus was originally addressing, and what topic was originally being discussed, we have to tread carefully. The tendency of the conservative is to take the whole dialogue as a blow-by-blow account of what actually happened in the life of Jesus. The tendency of the liberal, on the other hand, is to see this episode as a fiction created by the Johannine community in order to address the needs of the hour. Neither of these extremes is adequate. The real truth lies somewhere else.

In all probability the original dialogue bore close resemblance to the kind of controversy we see in Matthew 3.7–10, this time involving John the Baptist:

> But when John the Baptist saw many of the Pharisees and Sadducees coming to where he was baptising, he said to them: 'You brood of vipers! Who warned you to flee from the coming wrath? Produce fruit in keeping with repentance. And do not think you can say to yourselves, "We have Abraham as our father".'

In this incident, John the Baptist satirizes the Sadducees and Pharisees for their belief that Abrahamic descent was sufficient for salvation. Like Jesus in John 8.31f, John the Baptist uses the language of savage indignation. Like Jesus in John 8.31f, John the Baptist exposes the fallacy of relying on Abrahamic descent. In both texts, the protagonist is a prophetic satirist and the targets are groups who claim to be the children of Abraham.

It is more than probable that this incident involving the Baptist in Matt.3.7f is historical. As Davies and Allison have shown, the language of the Baptist here is consistent with his sayings elsewhere in the gospel. It is a Q saying characterized by Semitisms. It lacks distinctively Christian elements and it has parallels in the Qumran literature. As they put it:

> It is a good guess that disciples of John recalled their former master's words after they became followers of Jesus and that in this way the lines in Q found their way into the Jesus tradition.
>
> (Davies and Allison 1988: 301)

Returning to the fourth gospel, it is likely that Jesus also confronted similar groups in his own ministry and that John 8.31–59 preserves a good deal of material from such a controversy. It may well be that a group of Pharisees started on the road of discipleship with Jesus but then decided to let go of his teaching, to claim the sufficiency of Abrahamic descent and to revert to a life of obeying the Law. The plausibility of this hypothesis is greatly strengthened by the presence of language in John 8.31–59 which has similarities in the Synoptics. For example, the *ipsissima vox Iesou* ('the actual voice of Jesus') can still be heard in the parable of the son and the slave in John 8.35 (which resembles the domestic aura of some synoptic parables); the emphasis on the fatherhood of God in John 8.31f is also historical. Other parts of John 8.31–59 preserve what one might call the *ipsissima vox* of the original opponents, not least the charge that Jesus was a Samaritan and demon-possessed, which has parallels in Mark 3.22, Matthew 12.24, and Luke 11.15. In these and other matters, 'it seems that the mind of our evangelist is here moving among ideas which were represented in the most primitive tradition' (Dodd 1963: 332).

Having said that, it should also be stressed that this same controversy has been creatively redescribed in the light of controversies in the late first century church in which John was writing. A good deal of dramatic reinterpretation has taken place. Indeed, what J.L. Martyn proposes for John 9 could equally be proposed for John 8.31f, that it is a two-level drama reflecting both an incident in the ministry of the historical Jesus, *and* the Sitz im Leben of the persecuted Johannine community (Martyn 1979). At this second level, the 'Jews who had believed Jesus' might represent those Jewish Christians who were finding it hard to hold on to Jesus' teaching after the Jamnia edict. Perhaps this group were in danger of renouncing the Christian faith and becoming apostates. As Schnackenburg surmizes:

> We can ... reasonably assume that the evangelist has in mind Jewish Christians of his time who – perhaps as a result of Jewish counter-propaganda – are in danger of lapsing from faith in Christ.

> (Schnackenburg 1980: 204)

If this is true, then the violent language of John 8.31–59 would be explicable. John is using this dialogue as a means of warning Jewish Christians, in the strongest terms, that they must not become apostates.

Obviously this is a hypothetical reconstruction, but if it is correct it would help us to understand the 'communal origins and social function' of John 8.31–59. It would show how John has enlisted history for the purpose of social propoganda. Taking the material of his source, John has recast it as an informal satire which resonated with the experience of his readership. The tone, structure, setting and characterization of this episode all point to the kind of informal satire which was common in the early Christian era. Indeed, such informal satire was being perfected by the Roman poet Juvenal, *at exactly the same time as John was publishing the final version of his gospel at the end of the first century.* John therefore used a popular, developing literary genre and redescribed a heated controversy in his source so as to help his readers. These readers, in the main, had been cursed by Jamnia as apostates. The Jamnia edict had read, 'For the apostates let there be no hope. . . . Let the Nazarenes and the heretics be destroyed in a moment'. John responds to this curse by directing a strong attack against apostasy in his own church. Indeed, we might say that he curses apostates in a gospel intended for those who themselves had been cursed as apostates!

CONCLUSION

Having examined the polemic of Jesus in John 8.31–59 from both a literary and an historical perspective we are now in a position to engage in an ethical reading of our text. The necessity of such an approach is even more urgent where a text like John 8.31–59 employs informal satire of the most aggressive kind. Satire itself arises from those emotions which are generally regarded as the least admirable – anger, hatred, indignation and the like. It also evokes emotions which make most people feel uncomfortable – shame, anxiety, guilt, indignation. For this reason, satire is regarded as the basest kind of aesthetic expression. As Test puts it,

> The general attitude toward satire is comparable to that of members of a family toward a slightly disreputable relative, who though popular with the children makes some of the adults a bit uncomfortable.
>
> (Test 1991: 18)

In Jesus' satire of the apostate Jews we have on public display some of the least socially acceptable emotions, such as anger, righteousness, and savage indignation. An ethical reading of John 8.31–59 must therefore begin with a defence of the *saeva indignatio* which Jesus so overtly exhibits here. This is not as difficult as it appears. George Sand described indignation as 'the fiercest form of love'. It may just be that the satire of the apostate Jewish believers is an example of 'the fiercest form of love', of the kind of pastoral love that aims to shock potential defectors into an awakening. Indeed, my belief is that the intention of the author of John 8.31–59 was not only to record a controversy in the life of Jesus, but also to redescribe that controversy in such a way as to alert potential apostates in his own times to the dire consequences of falling away. Such disloyalty would engender the most severe kind of judgment from the Lord. It would be a sin against the community. To drive the point home John uses informal satire to dispel any illusion the potential apostate might have that his or her defection is justifiable. Such a strategy is an example of the fiercest form of pastoral love.

Jesus' language in John 8.31–59 is therefore language which can be defended on ethical and pastoral grounds. But this still leaves us with the abuse of this text throughout church history. What are we to do with a text which, irrespective of the original pastoral intention of its author, has been manifestly abused as an instrument of social and racial oppression? As Richard Lowry rightly says:

> In this broken world of human history, who can deny that there is an unbroken epigenous line of development from John's portrayal of the Jews as spawn of the devil, eagerly doing their 'father's desires'; through the woodcuts of 'the Jews and their father the devil'; up to a little children's picture book, published in 1936 by the Nazi's SturmerVerlag, whose first page is headed by the slogan: . . . 'the father of the Jews is the devil'?
>
> (Lawry 1977: 229)

It is a source of great sadness to me that a text which begins with a word of liberation should have been used throughout history as an instrument of oppression. John 8.31 begins:

> If you hold to my teaching, you are really my disciples. Then you will know the truth, and the truth will set you free. (8.31–32)

This is the language of liberation not of oppression. Furthermore, what follows these verses is not a satire of Judaism, intended to be used as a weapon of *Judenfeindschaft*. It is a satire of apostasy and a warning to Jewish Christians of the disastrous consequences of falling away in times of persecution. Indeed, in John 8.31–59 we have the same kind of severe warning against Christian apostasy which we find in Hebrews 6.4–6:

It is impossible for those who have once been enlightened, who have tasted the heavenly gift, who have shared in the Holy Spirit, who have tasted the goodness of the word of God and the powers of the coming age, if they fall away, to be brought back to repentance, because to their loss they are crucifying the Son of God all over again and subjecting him to public disgrace.

I can only speak as a Christian, but it seems to me that an ethical reading of John 8.31–59 requires a significant response from Christian readers; namely, repentance for abusing a text intended as a satire against apostasy, not against Judaism. The blame for this does not lie with the author, whose intention was pastoral and protective. The blame for this does not lie with the text, which is a satire of apostasy not of the Jewish people. The blame lies fairly and squarely on the shoulders of those who have interpreted John 8.31–59 with a prior commitment to anti-Semitism, and who have failed to see that this text is a condemnation not of 'the Jews' but of 'Jews who had believed Jesus' (8.31). Such an act of repentance, deriving from an awakening concerning the true literary and historical dynamics of this text, will never erase the memory of sins committed against the Jewish people. But with the appalling spectre of emerging anti-Semitism in Europe today, it would be at least one small step in the direction of justice for the Jewish people.

CONCLUSION

When I was studying English literature as my first degree, I remember participating in a seminar on Wordsworth's poem, 'She Dwelt Among the Untrodden Ways'. When we looked at it as a group of rather inexperienced students, I remember thinking that there was not a great deal I felt I could say about it. It was one of those poems where the diction was simple and the meaning crystal clear. In vain I cast my eyes over every line, seeking something insightful with which to impress my peers concerning the three verses:

> She dwelt among the untrodden ways
>   Beside the springs of Dove,
> A Maid whom there were none to praise
>   And very few to love;
>
> A violet by a mossy stone
>   Half hidden from the eye!
> – Fair as a star, when only one
>   Is shining in the sky.
>
> She lived unknown and few could know
>   When Lucy ceased to be:
> But she is in her grave, and, oh,
>   The difference to me!

As the discussion proceeded, the lecturer who was conducting the seminar began to tease out some unseen difficulties. He pointed out the paradoxes in the poem by asking various leading questions. 'How can a way be untrodden and still be a "way"? How can a maid be praised by none and yet, at the same time, loved by few? How can a person be both like a half-concealed flower and, at the same time, like a conspicuous star? How can a person live unknown and yet still be someone about whom a few could know?' As we continued, what began to dawn on us was the extraordinary combination of transparent simplicity and opaque profundity in Wordsworth's use of language. Here was a poet who knew how to use words in such a way that it was possible for the reader to stop short at a superficial reading. Here was a poet who knew how to explore 'differences' (see the last line) and to construct meanings which are 'half hidden from the eye' (line 6).

Writing this fifteen years on, it now seems to me that there are some broad similarities between John's use of language in the fourth gospel, and Wordsworth's use of language in the Lyrical Ballads. Both authors have created texts in which the diction is demotic, simple and accessible. Indeed, John's vocabulary is limited, repetitive and easily comprehensible. Yet, at the same time, both authors have managed to create meanings which are 'half hidden from the eye'. Wordsworth's poem, so apparently simple, is in reality an extraordinarily subtle exploration of paradox. John's gospel, also apparently simple, tells a story which is rich in terms of 'multivalence'. In other words, John constructs a narrative which is simple enough for a child to enjoy, and yet complex enough to have provoked the interest of the finest biblical scholars throughout history. It is, in the truest sense, a work of literature. If literary language is language which is self-consciously exploited for aesthetic purposes (and I am aware there is debate about that), then John's gospel surely qualifies as a work of literature. Whatever its original confessional purpose, John's gospel is a story which delights as well as instructs.

It is for this reason that the recent application of literary-critical methodologies to the fourth gospel shows such promise. After centuries of historical-critical studies which had begun to lose their momentum and freshness, these newer methods have now given fourth gospel research a new lease of life. Today the prospects look very hopeful. The pluralism of readings available to the modern scholar – deconstruction, rhetorical criticism, narrative criticism, ethical readings, feminist literary criticism, structuralism, liberation hermeneutics, political criticism, reader response criticism, and many more – presage a new dawn of scholarship both in John's gospel and in biblical criticism as a whole. Some of the articles and books which use such approaches on John's gospel have few insights which could not have been discovered using the older methods – such as historical criticism, form criticism, redaction criticism, source criticism, and the history of religions approach. That is partly due to the fact that the scholars who attempt such synchronic readings are not trained in the areas of literary theory and literary criticism. But where scholars have become thoroughly equipped in these two areas, and where the same scholars have sought to integrate literary methods with the older, historical approaches in their work, there is a good deal of interesting and perceptive scholarship emerging.

In this book I have attempted to introduce a wide range of readers to five different literary interpretations of aspects of John's gospel. In Chapter 1 I examined the hero of the gospel from a reader-response perspective, and demonstrated how the author and the narrator work together to create a character who is seductively elusive. In Chapter 2 I employed the structuralist, actantial model of narrative analysis (deriving from A.J. Greimas) on the plot of the fourth gospel, and in the process highlighted some of the half-hidden complexities of John's plot, counter-plot and micro-plots. In Chapter 3 I examined the genre of the gospel using Northrop Frye's archetypal approach to the modes of story-telling. There I tried to highlight the 'classic appeal' of the story with reference to the comic, romantic, ironic/satirical and tragic qualities in this extraordinary *Bios Iesou*. In Chapter 4 I exposed the style employed by the author using narrative criticism, a method which helps to elicit some of the characteristic literary devices of the gospel (characterization, structure, settings, plot, form, narrator, irony, symbolism and the like). In Chapter 5 I tried very hard to tackle the sensitive subject of John's polemic against 'the Jews', this time using a method known as 'the ethics of reception'.

In every chapter I have endeavoured to use not only these literary methodologies but also to ask and to answer questions posed by historically-minded critics. I have not treated the gospel story as a closed, autonomous world. I have taken very seriously the fact that the author was writing about an historical figure (Jesus of Nazareth) and that the gospel therefore has considerable value in terms of historical reference. I have also taken seriously the fact that this same author was building on narrative sources which circulated in and around his community (or communities) and that he drew upon these sources selectively. I have also taken seriously the fact that this author known as 'John' was writing for an ecclesial group with its own specific needs, and that the gospel both reflects those needs and seeks to meet them. In other words, I have endeavoured to produce readings which venerate the gospel as both literature *and* history. I have not gone down the road taken by some of my colleagues and treated the gospel as novelistic fiction.

In the final analysis, John's gospel is a magnificent work of literature but it is also much more. If the reader comes away from this study regarding the fourth gospel as 'a religious classic' I shall only be partially satisfied. Speaking from my own experience as a Christian minister, I feel bound to say that this narrative is of ultimate significance to all readers. If John's story of Jesus is true – in other words, 'true to history' and 'true to the real meaning of Jesus' – then it seems to me that one cannot come away from this gospel unaffected. The characterization of Pontius Pilate in John 18–19, so brilliantly carried off in so few words, illustrates once and for all the impossibility of neutrality when it comes to Jesus of Nazareth. To make no decision about Jesus is to decide against Jesus. This gospel presents all of us with the claim that we are in darkness until we come to the light, in death until we come to the Giver of Life. This gospel, in short, demands a *krisis*, a verdict, about Jesus. For those who accept the call of Jesus as an existential reality today, there is the promise of life in all its fullness. As the narrator points out:

> He came to that which was his own, but his own did not receive him. Yet to all who received him, to those who believed in his name, he gave the right to become the children of God – children born not of natural descent, nor of human decision, or a husband's will, but born of God.
>
> (John 1.11–13)

Further reading

LITERARY APPROACHES TO JOHN, 1980–93

Bartholomew, G. (1987) 'Feed my Lambs: John 21.15–19 as Oral Gospel', *Semeia* 39: 69–96.

Bauckham, R. (1993) 'The Beloved Disciple as Ideal Author', *JSNT* 49: 21–44.

Beutler, J. (1991) 'Zur Struktur von Johannes 6', *Studien zum Neuen Testament und seiner Umwelt* 16: 89–104.

Black, D. (1988) 'On the Style and Significance of John 17', *Criswell Theological Review* 3(1): 141–159.

Boers, H. (1980) 'Discourse Structure and Macro-structure in the Interpretation of Texts: Jn 4.1–42 as an Example', in Achtemeier, P. (ed.) *SBL 1980 Seminar Papers*, Chico, Scholars Press.

—— (1988) *Neither on this Mountain nor in Jerusalem. A study of John 4*, SBL Monograph Series no.35. Atlanta. Scholars Press.

Booth, S. (1992) 'Marking of Peak in the Gospel of John', *Notes Trans* 6(3): 18–26.

Born, J. (1988) 'Literary Features in the Gospel of John', *Direction* 17(2): 3–17.

Botha, J.E. (1990) 'Reader Entrapment as a Literary Device in John 4.1–42', *Neotestamentica* 24, 1: 37–47.

—— (1991) 'Jesus and the Samaritan Woman. A Speech Act Reading of John 4.1–42'. Supplements to *NovTest*. Vol. LXV. Leiden, E.J. Brill.

Braun, W. (1990) 'Resisting John: Ambivalent Redactor and Defensive Reader of the Fourth Gospel', *Studies in Religion/Sciences Religieuses* 19: 59–71.

Byrne, B. (1991) *Lazarus: A Contemporary Reading of John 11.1–46*, Collegeville, Minnesota: Liturgical Press.

Cahill, P. (1982) 'Narrative Art in John IV', *Religious Studies Bulletin* 2: 41–55.

Calloud, J. and Genuyt, F. (1985) *Le Discours d'adieu. Jean 13–17. Analyse Semiotique*, Lyon, Centre Thomas More.

—— (1987) *L'Evangile de Jean (II). Lecture Semiotique des chapitres 7 à 12*, L'Arbresle, Centre Thomas More.

—— (1989) *L'Evangile de Jean (I). Lecture Semiotique des chapitres 1 à 6*, L'Arbresle, Centre Thomas More.

Cook, C. (1991) '"I gotta use words when I talk to you": A literary examination of John', *New Blackfriars* 72: 365–376.

Cotterell, P. (1984) 'The Nicodemus Conversation: A Fresh Appraisal' *ExpTimes* 96: 237–242.

Culpepper, R.A. (1980) 'The Pivot of John's Prologue', *NTS* 27: 1–31.

—— (1990) 'Un example de commentaire fondé sur la critique narrative: Jean 5,1–18', in *La Communauté Johannique et son Histoire*, Geneva: Labor et Fides, pp.136–152.

—— (1991) 'The Johannine *Hypodeigma*: A Reading of John 13', Semeia 53: 133–152.

De Boer, M. (1992) 'Narrative Criticism, Historical Criticism, and the Gospel of John', *JSNT* 47: 35–48.

De Smidt, J. (1991) 'A Perspective on John 15.1–8', *Neotestamentica* 25(2): 251–272.

Dockery, D. (1988) 'Reading John 4.1–45. Some Diverse Hermeneutical Perspectives', *Criswell Theological Review* 3(1): 127–140.

—— (1988) 'John 9.1–41: A Narrative Discourse Study', *Occasional Papers in Translation and Textlinguistics* 2(2): 14–26.

Du Rand, J. (1982) *Die Struktuur van die christologie van die Evangelie van Johannes – metodologiese vorwegings*, Bloemfontein: Universiteit van die Oranje-Vrystaat.

—— (1985) 'The Characterization of Jesus as Depicted in the Narrative of the Fourth Gospel', *Neotestamentica* 19: 18–36.

—— (1986) 'Plot and Point of View in the Gospel of John', in Petzer J. and Hartin, P. (eds) *A South African Perspective on the New Testament*, Leiden, E.J. Brill.

—— (1990) 'Narratological Perspectives on John 13.1–38', *Hervormde Teologiese Studies* 46(3): 367–389.

—— (1991) 'A Syntactical and Narratological Reading of John 10 in Coherence with Chapter 9', in Buetler, J. and Fortna, R. (eds) *The Shepherd Discourse of John 10 and its Context*, Cambridge: Cambridge University Press.

—— (1991) 'Perspectives on Johannine Discipleship According to the Farewell Discourses', *Neotestamentica* 25(2): 311–325.

—— (1992) 'A Story and a Community: Reading the First Farewell Discourse (John 13.31–14.31) from Narratalogical and Sociological Perspective', *Neotestamentica* 26(1): 31–45.

Ellis, P. (1984) *The Genius of John: A Composition-Critical Commentary on the Fourth Gospel*, Collegeville, Minnesota: Liturgical Press.

Eslinger, L. (1987) 'The Wooing of the Woman at the Well: Jesus, the Reader and Reader-Response Criticism', *Lit. and Theology* 1: 167–183.

Foster, D. (1986) 'John Come Lately: The Belated Evangelist', in McConnell, F. (ed.) *The Bible and the Narrative Tradition*, Oxford: Oxford University Press.

Giblin, C. (1980) 'Suggestion, Negative Response and Positive Action in St John's Portrayal of Jesus', *NTS* 26: 197–211.

—— (1983) 'The Miraculous Crossing of the Sea (John 6.16–21)', *NTS* 29: 96–103.

—— (1984) 'Confrontations in John 18.1–27', *Biblica* 65: 210–231.

—— (1986) 'John's Narration of the Hearing before Pilate', *Biblica* 67: 221–239.

—— (1991) 'The Tripartite Narrative Structure of John's Gospel', *Biblica* 72: 449–468.

—— (1992) 'Mary's Anointing for Jesus' Burial-Resurrection (John 12.1–8)', *Biblica* 73: 560–564.

Girard, M. (1982) 'L'Unité de composition de Jean 6, au regard de l'analyse structurel', *L'Eglise et Theologie* 13: 79–110.

Hartman, L. (1984) 'An Attempt at a Text-Centred Exegesis of John 21', *Studia Theologia* 38: 29–45.

Henaut, B. (1990) 'John 4.43–54 and the Ambivalent Narrator', *Studies in Religion/Sciences Religieuses* 19: 287–304.

Kelber, W. (1987) 'The Authority of the Word in St John's Gospel: Charismatic Speech, Narrative Text, Logocentric Metaphysics', *Oral Tradition* 2: 108–131.

—— (1990) 'In the Beginning were the Words: The Apotheosis and Narrative Displacements of the Logos', *JAAR* 58: 69–98.

—— (1990) 'The Birth of a Beginning: John 1.1–18', *Semeia* 52: 121–144.

Kennedy, G. (1984) *New Testament Interpretation through Rhetorical Criticism*, Chapel Hill: University of North Carolina Press.

Kermode, F. (1986) 'St John as Poet', *JSNT* 28: 3–16.

—— (1987) 'John', in Kermode, F. and Alter, R (eds), *Literary Guide to the Bible*, London: Collins.

Kotzé, P. (1985) 'John and Reader's Response', *Neotestamentica* 19: 50–63.

Kurz, W. (1990) *Farewell Addresses in the New Testament*, Minnesota: Liturgical Press.

—— (1989) 'The Beloved Disciple and Implied Readers', *BTB* 19(3): 100–107.

Kysar, R. (1984) *John's Story of Jesus*, Philadelphia: Fortress Press.

—— (1991) 'Johannine Metaphor – Meaning and Function: A Literary Case Study of John 10.1–18', *Semeia* 53: 81–112.

Lemmer, H. (1991) 'A Possible Understanding by the Implied Reader, of Some of the Coming–Going–Being–Sent Pronouncements, in the Johannine Farewell Discourses', *Neotestamentica* 25(2): 289–310.

Liebert, E. (1984) 'That you may Believe: The Fourth Gospel and Structural Developmental Theory', *BTB* 14: 67–73.

Lombard, H. and Oliver, W. (1991) 'A Working Supper in Jerusalem: John 13.1–38: introduces Jesus' Farewell Discourses', *Neotestamentica* 25(2): 357–378.

Mlakuzhyil, G. (1987) *The Christocentric Literary Structure of the Fourth Gospel*, Rome: Pontificio Instituto Biblico.

Moloney, F. (1986) 'The Structure and Message of John 13.1–38', *Australian Biblical Review* 34: 1–16.

—— (1987) 'The Structure and Message of John 15.1–16.3', *Australian Biblical Review* 35: 35–49.

—— (1990) 'Reading John 2.13–22: The Purification of the Temple', *Revue Biblique* 97: 432–452.

—— (1991) 'A Sacramental Reading of John 13.1–38', *CBQ* 53: 237–256.

—— (1992). 'Who is "the Reader" in/of the Fourth Gospel?' *Australian Biblical Review* 40: 20–33.

—— (1993) *Belief in the Word. Reading the Fourth Gospel: John 1–4*, Minneapolis, Minnesota: Fortress Press.

Moore, S. (1989) 'Rifts in (a reading of) the Fourth Gospel, or: does Johannine Irony still Collapse in a Reading that Draws Attention to Itself', *Neotestamentica* 23(1): 5–17.

—— (1993) 'Are There Impurities in the Living Water that the Johannine Jesus Dispenses? Deconstruction, Feminism, and the Samaritan Woman', *Biblical Interpretation* 1(2): 207–227.

Neyrey, J. (1990) 'Jesus the Judge: Forensic Process in John 8.21–59', *Biblica* 71: 509–541.

Nicholson, G. (1983) *Death as Departure*, Chico, California: Scholars Press.

Nortje, S. (1986) 'The Role of Women in the Fourth Gospel', *Neotestamentica* 20: 21–28.

O'Day, G. (1986) *Revelation in the Fourth Gospel: Narrative Mode and Theological Claim*, Philadelphia: Fortress Press.

—— (1988) *The Word Disclosed. John's Story and Narrative Preaching*, St Louis, Missouri: CBP Press.

—— (1991) '"I have overcome the world" (John 16.33): Narrative Time in John 13–17', *Semeia* 53: 153–166.

—— (1992) 'John 7.53–8.11: A Study in Misreading', *JBL* 111: 631–640.

Ostenstad, G. (1991) 'The Structure of the Fourth Gospel: Can it be Defined Objectively?' *Studia Theologica* 45(1): 33–55.

Pamment, M. (1985) 'Focus in the Fourth Gospel', *ExpTimes* 97: 71–75.

Panier, L. (1992) 'Cana et le Temple: la pratique et la théorie: Une lecture Semiotique de Jean 2', *LumVie* 41: 37–54.

Patte, D. (1983) 'Narrative and Discourse in Structural Exegesis: John 6 and I Thessalonians', *Semeia* 26: 85–102.

—— (1990) *Structural Exegesis for New Testament Critics*, Minneapolis: Fortress Press.

Phillips, G. (1983) 'This is a Hard Saying. Who can be a Listener to it?': Creating a Reader in John 6', *Semeia* 26: 23–56.

Reinhartz, A. (1989) 'Great Expectations: A Reader-oriented Approach to Johannine Christology and Eschatology', *Lit. and Theology* 3: 61–76.

—— (1989) 'Jesus as Prophet: Predictive Prolepses in the Fourth Gospel', *JSNT* 36: 3–16.

—— (1993) *The Word in the World. The Cosmological Tale in the Fourth Gospel*, Alpharetta, Georgia: Scholars Press.

Resseguie, J. (1982) 'John 9: A Literary-Critical Analysis', in Gros Louis, K. (ed.) *Literary Interpretations of Biblical Narratives*, Vol.II, Nashville, Tennessee: Abingdon Press.

Richard, E. (1985) 'Expressions of Double Meaning and their Function in the Gospel of John', *NTS* 31: 96–112.

Rissi, M. (1983) 'Der Aufbau des vierten Evangeliums', *NTS* 29: 48–54.

Schenk, W. (1992) 'Interne Strukturierungen Schluss-Segment Johannes 21', *NTS* 38: 507–530.

Schenke, L. (1992) *Das Johannesevangelium. Einführung – Text – Dramatische Gestalt*, Cologne: Kohlhammer.

Schneiders, S. (1982) 'Women in the Fourth Gospel and the Role of Women in the Contemporary Church', *BTB* 12(2): 35–45.

Schram, T. (1990) 'The Logical Structure of John's Gospel', *Notes on Translation* 4(1): 24–30.

Segovia, F. (1985) 'The Structure, *Tendenz* and *Sitz im Leben* of John 13.31–14.31', *JBL* 104: 471–493.

—— (1991) *The Farewell of the Word. The Johannine Call to Abide*, Minneapolis, Minnesota: Fortress Press.

—— (1991) 'The Final Farewell of Jesus: A Reading of John 20.30–21.25', *Semeia* 53: 167–190.

—— (1991) 'Towards a New Direction in Johannine Scholarship: The Fourth Gospel from a Literary Perspective', *Semeia* 53: 1–22.

—— (1993) *The Prayer of the Word: A Johannine Call to Unity*, Minneapolis, Minnesota: Fortress Press.

Senior, D. (1991) *The Passion of Jesus in the Gospel of John*, Leominster, UK: Gracewing.

Simoens, Y. (1981) *La Gloire D'Aimer: Structures Stylistiques et Interprétatives dans le Discours de Cène (Jn 13–17)*, Rome: Biblical Institute Press.

Staley, J. (1986) *The Print's First Kiss: A Rhetorical Investigation of the Implied Reader in the Fourth Gospel*, Atlanta, Georgia: Scholars Press.

—— (1986) 'The Structure of John's Prologue: its Implications for the Gospel's Narrative Structure', *CBQ* 48: 241–264.

—— (1993) 'Subversive Narrative – Victimized Reader: A Reader Response Assessment of a Text-Critical Problem, John 18.12–24', *JSNT* 51: 79–98.

Stibbe, M. (1993) 'Return to Sender: A Structuralist Approach to John's Gospel', *Biblical Interpretation* 1(2): 189–206.

Talbert, C.H. (1992) *Reading John. A Literary and Theological Commentary*, New York: Crossroad.

Theissen, K. (1990) 'Jesus and Women in the Gospel of John', *Direction* 19(2): 52–64.

Theron, S. (1987) 'A Multi-Faceted Approach to an Important Thrust in the Prayer of Jesus in John 17', *Neotestamentica* 21(1): 77–94.

Thompson, M. (1988) *The Humanity of Jesus in the Fourth Gospel*, Philadelphia: Fortress Press.

Thyen, H. (1987) 'Johannesbriefe', *Theologische Realenzyklopadie* 17: 186–200.

—— (1987) 'Johannesevangelium', *Theologische Realenzyklopadie* 17: 200–225.

Tolmie, D. (1991) 'The Function of Focalisation in John 13–17', *Neotestamentica* 25(2): 273–287.

Trudinger, P. (1992) 'Of Women, Weddings, Wells, Waterpots and Wine! Reflections on Johannine Themes (John 2.1–11 and 4.1–42)', *St Mark's Review* 151: 10–16.

Van Aarde, A. (1991) 'Narrative Criticism Applied to John 4.43–54', in Hartin, P. and Petzer, J. (eds) *Text and Interpretation: New Approaches in the Criticism of the New Testament*, Leiden: E.J. Brill.

Van Belle, G. (1985) *Les Parenthèses dans L'Evangile de Jean*, Leuven: Peeters.

Van den Heever, G. (1992) 'Theological Metaphorics and the Metaphors of John's Gospel', *Neotestamentica* 26(1): 89–100.

Van Tilborg, S. (1989) 'The Gospel of John: Communicative Processes in a Narrative Text', *Neotestamentica* 23: 19–27.

—— (1991) 'Ideology and Text: John 15 in the Context of the Farewell Discourse', in Hartin, P. and Petzer, J. (eds) *Text and Interpretation: New Approaches in the Criticism of the New Testament*, Leiden: E.J. Brill.

—— (1993) *Imaginative Love in John*, Leiden: E.J. Brill.

Von Wahlde, U. (1984) 'Literary Structure and Theological Argument in Three Discourses with the Jews in the Fourth Gospel', *JBL* 103: 575–584.

Webster, E. (1982) 'Pattern in the Fourth Gospel', in Clines, D. and Gunn, D. (eds) *Art and Meaning*, Sheffield: JSOT Press.

Wendland, E. (1992) 'Rhetoric of the Word. An Interactional Discourse Analysis of the Lord's Prayer of John 17 and its Communicative Implications', *Neotestamentica* 26(1): 59–88.

Wiarda, T. (1992) 'John 21.1–23: Narrative Unity and its Implications', *JSNT* 46: 53–71.

Wuellner, W. (1991) 'Putting Life back into the Lazarus Story and its Reading: The Narrative Rhetoric of John 11 as the Narration of Faith', *Semeia* 53: 113–131.

—— (1991) 'Rhetorical Criticism and its Theory in Culture-Critical Perspective: The Narrative Rhetoric of John 11', in Hartin, P. and Petzer, J. (eds) *Text and Interpretation: New Approaches in Criticism of the New Testament*, Leiden: E.J. Brill.

References

Alter, R. (1981) *The Art of Biblical Narrative*, New York: Basic Books.

Aune, D. (1987) *The New Testament in its Literary Environment*, Philadelphia: Westminster Press.

Bar-Efrat, S. (1989) *Narrative Art in the Bible*, Sheffield: Almond Press.

Barrett, C.K. (1978) *The Gospel According to St John*, London: SPCK.

Barthes, R. (1977) 'The Struggle with the Angel', in *Image Music Text* (trans. Stephen Heath), London: Fontana.

Bodkin, M. (1978) *Archetypal Patterns in Poetry*, Oxford: Oxford University Press (first published by Oxford University Press in 1934).

Botha, E. (1990) 'John 4.16a: A Difficult Text Speech Act Theoretically Revisited', *Scriptura* 35: 1–9.

—— (1991a) 'The Case of Johannine Irony Reopened I: The Problematic Current Situation', *Neotestamentica* 25(2): 209–220.

—— (1991b) 'The Case of Johannine Irony Reopened II: Suggestions, Alternative Approaches', *Neotestamentica* 25(2): 221–232.

Bowen, C. (1930) 'The Fourth Gospel as Dramatic Material', *JBL* 49: 292–305.

Bultmann, R. (1971) *The Gospel of John: A Commentary* (translated from the 1941 German edition by G.R. Beasley Murray *et al.*), Oxford: Basil Blackwell.

Burridge, R. (1990) 'Genre', in Coggins, R. and Houlden, L. (eds) *A Dictionary of Biblical Interpretation*, London: SCM Press.

—— (1992) *What are the Gospels?*, Cambridge: Cambridge University Press (SNTS monograph series no. 70).

Clavier, H. (1959) 'Ironie dans le Quatrième Evangile', in Aland, K. (ed.) *Studia Evangelica*, Berlin: Akademie.

Cohn-Sherbok, D. (1992) *The Crucified Jew: Twenty Centuries of Christian Anti-Semitism*, London: Harper Collins.

Collingwood, R. (1953) *The Idea of History*, Oxford: Oxford University Press.

Connick, M. (1948) 'The Dramatic Character of the Fourth Gospel', *JBL* 67: 159–169.

Crossan, J.D. (1979) 'It is Written: A Structuralist Analysis of John 6', in Achetemeier, P. (ed.) *Society of Biblical Literature: 1979 Seminar Papers*, Missoula, Montana: Scholars Press.

Culpepper, R.A. (1983) *Anatomy of the Fourth Gospel: A Study in Literary Design*, Philadelphia: Fortress Press.

—— (1987) 'The Gospel of John and the Jews', *Review and Expositor* 84: 273–288.

Davies, M. (1992) *Rhetoric and Reference in the Fourth Gospel*, Sheffield: Sheffield Academic Press.

Davies, W.D. and Allison, D.C. (1988) *The Gospel According to St Matthew. Vol.I*, Edinburgh: T & T. Clark.

De Jonge, M. (1977) *Jesus: Stranger from Heaven and Son of God*, Missoula, Montana: Scholars Press.

Dodd, C.H. (1928) *The Authority of the Bible*, London: Nisbet & Co.

—— (1963) *Historical Tradition in the Fourth Gospel*, Cambridge: Cambridge University Press.

—— (1965) *The Interpretation of the Fourth Gospel*, Cambridge: Cambridge University Press.

Domeris, W. (1983) 'The Johannine Drama', *Journal of Theology for Southern Africa* 42: 29–35.

Downing, G. (1990) 'Hellenism', in Coggins, R. and Houlden, L. (eds) *The Dictionary of Biblical Interpretation*, London: SCM Press.

Duke, P. (1985) *Irony in the Fourth Gospel*, Atlanta: John Knox Press.

Edwards, H.E. (1953) *The Disciple Who Wrote These Things*, London: Clarke.

Flanagan, N. (1981) 'The Gospel of John as Drama', *Bible Today* 19: 264–270.

Frye, N. (1971) *Anatomy of Criticism*, Princeton: Princeton University Press.

Greimas, A.J. (1966) *Semantique Structurale*, Paris: Larousse.

Hitchcock, F. (1911) *A Fresh Study of the Fourth Gospel*, London: SPCK.

—— (1923) 'Is the Fourth Gospel a Drama?' *Theology* 7: 307–17.

Iser, W. (1974) *The Implied Reader. Patterns of Communication in Prose Fiction from Bunyan to Beckett*, Baltimore and London: Johns Hopkins University Press.

Jemielity, T. (1992) *Satire and the Hebrew Prophets*, Westminster: John Knox Press.

Kermode, F. (1979) *Genesis of Secrecy*, Cambridge, Massachusetts: Harvard University Press.

Kernan, A. (1959) *The Cankered Muse. Satire of the English Renaissance*, New Haven: Yale University Press.

Kotzé, P. (1985) 'Ironie in die Johannesevangelie', *Hervormde Teologiese Studies* 43: 431–447.

Lee, E. (1953) 'The Drama of the Fourth Gospel', *ExpTimes* 65: 173–176.

Lewis, C.S. (1979) *Preface to Paradise Lost*, Oxford: Oxford University Press (1st edition, 1942).

Lindars, B. (1971) *Behind the Fourth Gospel*, London: SPCK.

Lowry, R. (1977) 'The Rejected-Suitor Syndrome: Human Sources of New Testament "Antisemitism"', *Journal of Ecumenical Studies* 14.

MacRae, G. (1993) 'Theology and Irony in the Fourth Gospel' in Stibbe, M. (ed.) *The Gospel of John as Literature: An Anthology of Twentieth Century Perspectives*, Leiden: E.J. Brill.

Malina, B. (1985) 'The Gospel of John in Sociolinguistic Perspective', in

Waetjen, H. (ed.) *48th Colloquy of the Center for Hermeneutical Studies*, Berkeley, California: Center for Hermeneutical Studies.

Martyn, J. (1979) *History and Theology in the Fourth Gospel*, Nashville, Tennessee: Abingdon Press (first published by Abingdon Press in 1968).

Meeks, W. (1972) 'The Man from Heaven in Johannine Sectarianism', *JBL* 91: 44–72.

Mink, L. (1970) 'History and Fiction as Modes of Representation'. *New Literary History* 1: 541–548.

Muilenburg, J. (1932) 'Literary Form in the Fourth Gospel', *JBL* 51: 40–53.

Myers, D. (1988) 'Irony and Humour in the Gospel of John'. *Occasional Papers in Translation and Textlinguistics* 2(2): 1–13.

Neyrey, J. (1988) *An Ideology of Revolt. John's Christology in Social-Science Perspective*, Philadelphia: Fortress Press.

Noakes, D. (1987) *Raillery and Rage. A Study of Eighteenth Century Satire*, Brighton, Sussex: Harvester Press.

Nuttall, A. (1980) *Overheard by God: Fiction and Prayer in Herbert, Milton, Dante and St John*, London: Methuen.

O'Day, G. (1986) 'Narrative Mode and Theological Claim: A Study in the Fourth Gospel', *JBL* 105(4): 657–668.

Pierce, E. (1960) 'The Fourth Gospel as Drama', *Religion in Life* 29: 453–455.

Robinson, J. (1985) *The Priority of John*, London: SCM Press.

Ruckstuhl, E. (1951) *Die literarische Einheit des Johannesevangeliums*, Freiburg: Paulus Press.

Ryken, L. (1974) *The Literature of the Bible*, Grand Rapids, Michigan: Zondervan Publishing House.

Schnackenburg, R. (1980) *The Gospel According to St John, Vol.II*, New York: Herder & Herder.

Schweizer, E. (1939) *Ego Eimi*, Gottingen: Vandenhoeck.

Segovia, F. (1991) 'The Journey(s) of the Word of God', *Semeia* 53: 23–54.

Staley, J. (1991) 'Stumbling in the Dark, Reaching for the Light: Reading Character in John 5 and 9', *Semeia* 53: 55–80.

Sternberg, M. (1985) *The Poetics of Biblical Narrative*, Bloomington, Indiana: Indiana University Press.

Stibbe, M. (1991) 'The Elusive Christ: A New Reading of the Fourth Gospel'. *JSNT* 44: 20–39.

—— (1992) *John as Storyteller: Narrative Criticism and the Fourth Gospel*, Cambridge: Cambridge University Press (SNTS monograph series no. 73).

—— (1993a) *John. Readings: A New Biblical Commentary*, Sheffield: Sheffield Academic Press.

—— (ed.) (1993b) *The Gospel of John as Literature. An Anthology of Twentieth Century Perspectives*, Leiden: E.J. Brill.

—— (1994) 'A Tomb with a View: John 11.1–44 in Narrative-Critical Focus', *NTS* 40: 38–54.

Test, G. (1991) *Satire. Spirit and Art*, Tampa: University of South Florida Press.

Theissen, G. (1987) *The Shadow of the Galilean*, London: SCM Press.

Tillyard, E. (1969) (ed.) *Paradise Lost* (Milton), London: George Harrap & Co.

Tracy, D. (1981) *The Analogical Imagination*, London: SCM Press.

Von Wahlde, U. (1982) 'The Johannine Jews: A Critical Survey', *NTS* 28: 33–60.

Wead, D. (1970) *Literary Devices in John's Gospel*, Basle: Friedrich Reinhart Kommissionsverlag.

—— (1974) 'Johannine Irony as a Key to the Author-Audience Relationship in John's Gospel', in Francis, F. (ed.) *American Academy of Religion, Biblical Literature: 1974*, Missoula: Scholars Press.

White, H. (1973) *Metahistory*, London: Johns Hopkins University Press.

—— (1978) 'The Historical Text as Literary Artifact', in Canary, R. (ed.) *The Writing of History*, Madison, Wisconsin: Wisconsin University Press.

Windisch, H. (1923) 'John's Narrative Style', (trans. D. Orton) in Stibbe, M. (ed.) *The Gospel of John as Literature: An Anthology of Twentieth Century Perspectives*, Leiden: E.J. Brill.

Young, F. (1993) 'Allegory and the Ethics of Reading', in Watson, F. (ed.) *The Open Text. New Directions to Biblical Studies?*, London: SCM Press.

Index